DISCOURSES IN AMERICA

DISCOURSES IN AMERICA

BY

MATTHEW ARNOLD

London

MACMILLAN AND CO., Ltd.

NEW YORK : THE MACMILLAN CO.

1896

Republished, 1970
Scholarly Press, 22929 Industrial Drive East
St. Clair Shores, Michigan 48080

Library of Congress Catalog Card Number: 76-131610
Standard Book Number 403-00497-7

This edition is printed on a high-quality,
acid-free paper that meets specification
requirements for fine book paper referred
to as "300-year" paper

PREFACE

OF the three discourses in this volume, the second was originally given as the Rede Lecture at Cambridge, was recast for delivery in America, and is reprinted here as so recast. The first discourse, that on 'Numbers,' was originally given in New York. It was afterwards published in the *Nineteenth Century*, and I have to thank Mr. Knowles for kindly permitting me to reprint it now. The third discourse, that on

'Emerson,' was originally given in Emerson's 'own delightful town,' Boston.

I am glad of every opportunity of thanking my American audiences for the unfailing attention and kindness with which they listened to a speaker who did not flatter them, who would have flattered them ill, but who yet felt, and in fact expressed, more esteem and admiration than his words were sometimes, at a hasty first hearing, supposed to convey. I cannot think that what I have said of Emerson will finally be accounted scant praise, although praise universal and unmixed it certainly is not. What high esteem I feel for the suitableness and easy play of American institutions I have

had occasion, since my return home,
to say publicly and emphatically.
But nothing in the discourse on
'Numbers' was at variance with this
high esteem, although a caution,
certainly, was suggested. But then
some caution or other, to be drawn
from the inexhaustibly fruitful truth
that moral causes govern the standing
and the falling of States, who is there
that can be said not to need?

All need it, we in this country need
it, as indeed in the discourse on
'Numbers I have by an express
instance shown. Yet as regards us
in this country at the present moment,
I am tempted, I confess, to resort to
the great truth in question, not for caution so much as for consolation. Our

politics are 'battles of the kites and
the crows,' of the Barbarians and the
Philistines; each combatant striving to
affirm himself still, while all the vital
needs and instincts of our national
growth demand, not that either of the
combatants should be enabled to affirm
himself, but that each should be transformed. Our aristocratical class, the
Barbarians, have no perception of the
real wants of the community at home.
Our middle classes, the great Philistine power, have no perception of our
real relations to the world abroad, no
clue, apparently, for guidance, where-
ever that attractive and ever-victorious
rhetorician, who is the Minister of their
choice, may take them, except the for-
mula of that submissive animal which

carried the prophet Balaam. Our
affairs are in the condition which,
from such parties to our politics,
might be expected. Yet amid all the
difficulties and mortifications which
beset us, with the Barbarians impossible, with the Philistines determining
our present course, with our rising
politicians seeking only that the mind
of the Populace, when the Populace
arrives at power, may be found in
harmony with the mind of Mr. Carvell
Williams, which they flatter themselves they have fathomed; with the
House of Lords a danger, and the
House of Commons a scandal, and
the general direction of affairs infelicitous as we see it,—one consolation remains to us, and that no slight

or unworthy one. Infelicitous the
general direction of our affairs may
be; but the individual Englishman,
whenever and wherever called upon to
do his duty, does it almost invariably
with the old energy, courage, virtue.
And this is what we gain by having
had, as a people, in the ground of
our being, a firm faith in conduct; by
having believed, more steadfastly and
fervently than most, this great law that
moral causes govern the standing and
the falling of men and nations. The
law gradually widens, indeed, so as to
include light as well as honesty and
energy; to make light, also, a moral
cause. Unless we are transformed
we cannot finally stand, and without
more light we cannot be transformed.

But in the trying hours through which before our transformation we have to pass, it may well console us to rest our thoughts upon our life's law even as we have hitherto known it, and upon all which even in our present imperfect acception of it it has done for us.

CONTENTS

NUMBERS;

OR

THE MAJORITY AND THE REMNANT

THERE is a characteristic saying of Dr.
Johnson : ' Patriotism is the last refuge
of a scoundrel.'   The saying is cynical,
many will even call it brutal ; yet it
has in it something of plain, robust
sense and truth.   We do often see
men passing themselves off as patriots,
who are in truth scoundrels ; we meet
with talk and proceedings laying claim
to patriotism, which are these gentlemen's last refuge.   We may all of us

agree in praying to be delivered from patriots and patriotism of this sort. Short of such, there is undoubtedly, sheltering itself under the fine name of patriotism, a good deal of self-flattery and self-delusion which is mischievous. 'Things are what they are, and the consequences of them will be what they will be; why, then, should we desire to be deceived?' In that uncompromising sentence of Bishop Butler's is surely the right and salutary maxim for both individuals and nations.

Yet there is an honourable patriotism which we should satisfy if we can, and should seek to have on our side. At home I have said so much of the characters of our society and the

prospects of our civilisation, that I
can hardly escape the like topic elsewhere. Speaking in America, I cannot well avoid saying something about
the prospects of society in the United
States. It is a topic where one is apt
to touch people's patriotic feelings.
No one will accuse me of having
flattered the patriotism of that great
country of English people on the other
side of the Atlantic, amongst whom I
was born. Here, so many miles from
home, I begin to reflect with tender
contrition, that perhaps I have not,—
I will not say flattered the patriotism
of my own countrymen enough, but
regarded it enough. Perhaps that is
one reason why I have produced so
very little effect upon them. It was

a fault of youth and inexperience.
But it would be unpardonable to come
in advanced life and repeat the same
error here. You will not expect im-
possibilities of me. You will not
expect me to say that things are not
what, in my judgment, they are, and
that the consequences of them will not
be what they will be. I should make
nothing of it; I should be a too
palpable failure. But I confess that
I should be glad if in what I say
here I could engage American patriotism on my side, instead of rous-
ing it against me. And it so hap-
pens that the paramount thoughts
which your great country raises in
my mind are really and truly of a
kind to please, I think, any true

American patriot, rather than to offend him.

The vast scale of things here, the extent of your country, your numbers, the rapidity of your increase, strike the imagination, and are a common topic for admiring remark. Our great orator, Mr. Bright, is never weary of telling us how many acres of land you have at your disposal, how many bushels of grain you produce, how many millions you are, how many more millions you will be presently, and what a capital thing this is for you. Now, though I do not always agree with Mr. Bright, I find myself agreeing with him here. I think your numbers afford a very real and important ground for satisfaction.

Not that your great numbers, or
indeed great numbers of men anywhere, are likely to be all good, or
even to have the majority good.
'The majority are bad,' said one of
the wise men of Greece; but he was a
pagan.　Much to the same effect, however, is the famous sentence of the
New Testament: 'Many are called,
few chosen.'　This appears a hard
saying; frequent are the endeavours
to elude it, to attenuate its severity.
But turn it how you will, manipulate
it as you will, the few, as Cardinal
Newman well says, can never mean
the many.　Perhaps you will say that
the majority *is*, sometimes, good; that
its impulses are good generally, and its
action is good occasionally.　Yes, but

it lacks principle, it lacks persistence;
if to-day its good impulses prevail,
they succumb to-morrow; sometimes
it goes right, but it is very apt to
go wrong. Even a popular orator, or
a popular journalist, will hardly say
that the multitude may be trusted to
have its judgment generally just, and
its action generally virtuous. It may
be better, it is better, that the body of
the people, with all its faults, should
act for itself, and control its own
affairs, than that it should be set
aside as ignorant and incapable, and
have its affairs managed for it by a
so-called superior class, possessing
property and intelligence. Property
and intelligence cannot be trusted to
show a sound majority themselves;

the exercise of power by the people tends to educate the people. But still, the world being what it is, we must surely expect the aims and doings of the majority of men to be at present very faulty, and this in a numerous community no less than in a small one. So much we must certainly, I think, concede to the sages and to the saints.

Sages and saints are apt to be severe, it is true; apt to take a gloomy view of the society in which they live, and to prognosticate evil to it. But then it must be added that their prognostications are very apt to turn out right. Plato's account of the most gifted and brilliant community of the ancient world, of that

Athens of his to which we all owe
so much, is despondent enough.
'There is but a very small remnant,'
he says, 'of honest followers of wisdom, and they who are of these few,
and who have tasted how sweet and
blessed a possession is wisdom, and
who can fully see, moreover, the mad-
ness of the multitude, and that there
is no one, we may say, whose action
in public matters is sound, and no ally
for whosoever would help the just,
what,' asks Plato, 'are they to do?
They may be compared,' says Plato,
'to a man who has fallen among wild
beasts; he will not be one of them,
but he is too unaided to make head
against them; and before he can do
any good to society or his friends,

he will be overwhelmed and perish
uselessly.   When he considers this,
he will resolve to keep still, and to
mind his own business; as it were
standing aside under a wall in a storm
of dust and hurricane of driving wind;
and he will endure to behold the
rest filled with iniquity, if only he
himself may live his life clear of injustice and of impiety, and depart,
when his time comes, in mild and
gracious mood, with fair hope.'

Plato's picture here of democratic
Athens is certainly gloomy enough.
We may be sure the mass of his
contemporaries would have pro-
nounced it to be monstrously over-
charged.   We ourselves, if we had
been living then, should most of us

have by no means seen things as
Plato saw them. No, if we had seen
Athens even nearer its end than
when Plato wrote the strong words
which I have been quoting, Athens
in the very last days of Plato's life,
we should most of us probably have
considered that things were not going
badly with Athens. There is a long
sixteen years' administration,—the
administration of Eubulus,—which
fills the last years of Plato's life, and
the middle years of the fourth century
before Christ. A temperate German
historian thus describes Athens during
this ministry of Eubulus : 'The grand-
eur and loftiness of Attic democracy
had vanished, while all the pernicious
germs contained in it were fully de-

veloped. A life of comfort and a
craving for amusement were en-
couraged in every way, and the interest of the citizens was withdrawn
from serious things. Conversation
became more and more superficial
and frivolous. Famous courtesans
formed the chief topic of talk; the
new inventions of Thearion, the
leading pastry-cook in Athens, were
hailed with loud applause; and the
witty sayings which had been uttered
in gay circles were repeated about
town as matters of prime importance.'

No doubt, if we had been living
then to witness this, we should from
time to time have shaken our heads
gravely, and said how sad it all was.
But most of us would not, I think,

have been very seriously disquieted
by it.   On the other hand, we should
have found many things in the Athens
of Eubulus to gratify us.   'The democrats,' says the same historian whom
I have just quoted, 'saw in Eubulus
one of their own set at the head of
affairs;' and I suppose no good
democrat would see that without
pleasure.   Moreover, Eubulus was of
popular character.   In one respect he
seems to have resembled your own
'heathen Chinee'; he had 'guileless
ways,' says our historian, 'in which the
citizens took pleasure.'   He was also
a good speaker, a thorough man of
business; and, above all, he was very
skilful in matters of finance.   His
administration was both popular and

prosperous.   We should certainly have
said, most of us, if we had encountered
somebody announcing his resolve to
stand aside under a wall during such
an administration, that he was a goose
for his pains; and if he had called it
'a falling among wild beasts' to have
to live with his fellow-citizens who had
confidence in Eubulus, their country,
and themselves, we should have
esteemed him very impertinent.

Yes;—and yet at the close of that
administration of Eubulus came the
collapse, and the end of Athens as an
independent State.   And it was to
the fault of Athens herself that the
collapse was owing.   Plato was right
after all; the majority were bad, and
the remnant were impotent

So fared it with that famous Athenian State, with the brilliant people
of art and intellect.   Now let us turn
to the people of religion.   We have
heard Plato speaking of the very
small remnant which honestly sought
wisdom.   *The remnant!*—it is the
word of the Hebrew prophets also,
and especially is it the word of the
greatest of them all, Isaiah.   Not
used with the despondency of Plato,
used with far other power informing
it, and with a far other future await-
ing it, filled with fire, filled with
hope, filled with faith, filled with joy,
this term itself, *the remnant*, is yet
Isaiah's term as well as Plato's.   The
texts are familiar to all Christendom.
' Though thy people Israel be as the

sand of the sea, only a remnant of them shall return.' Even this remnant, a tenth of the whole, if so it may be, shall have to come back into the purging fire, and be again cleared and further reduced there. But nevertheless, 'as a terebinth tree, and as an oak, whose substance is in them, though they be cut down, so the stock of that burned tenth shall be a holy seed.'

Yes, the small remnant should be a holy seed; but the great majority, as in democratic Athens, so in the kingdoms of the Hebrew nation, were unsound, and their State was doomed. This was Isaiah's point. The actual commonwealth of the 'drunkards' and the 'blind,' as he calls them, in Israel and Judah, of the dissolute grandees and gross and foolish common people, of the great majority, must perish; its perishing was the necessary stage towards a happier future. And Isaiah was right, as Plato was right. No doubt to most of us, if we had been there to see it, the kingdom of Ephraim or of Judah, the society of Samaria and Jerusalem, would have seemed to contain a great deal else besides dissolute grandees and foolish common people. No doubt we should have thought parts of their policy serious, and some of their alliances promising. No doubt, when we read the Hebrew prophets now, with the larger and more patient temper of

a different race and an augmented
experience, we often feel the blame
and invective to be too absolute.
Nevertheless, as to his grand point,
Isaiah, I say, was right. The majority in the Jewish State, whatever they
might think or say, whatever their
guides and flatterers might think or
say, the majority were unsound, and
their unsoundness must be their ruin.

Isaiah, however, does not make his
remnant confine itself, like Plato's, to
standing aside under a wall during
this life and then departing in mild
temper and good hope when the time
for departure comes ; Isaiah's remnant
saves the State. Undoubtedly he
means to represent it as doing so.
Undoubtedly he imagines his Prince

of the house of David who is to be
born within a year's time, his royal
and victorious Immanuel, he imagines
him witnessing as a child the chastisement of Ephraim and the extirpation
of the bad majority there; then witnessing as a youth the chastisement
of Judah and the extirpation of the
bad majority there also; but finally,
in mature life, reigning over a State
renewed, preserved, and enlarged, a
greater and happier kingdom of the
chosen people.

Undoubtedly Isaiah conceives his
remnant in this wise; undoubtedly
he imagined for it a part which, in
strict truth, it did not play, and could
not play. So manifest was the non-
fulfilment of his prophecy, taken

strictly, that ardent souls feeding
upon his words had to wrest them
from their natural meaning, and to
say that Isaiah directly meant something which he did not directly mean.
Isaiah, like Plato, with inspired insight foresaw that the world before
his eyes, the world of actual life, the
State and city of the unsound majority, could not stand. Unlike Plato,
Isaiah announced with faith and joy
a leader and a remnant certain to
supersede them. But he put the
leader's coming, and he put the success of the leader's and the remnant's
work, far, far too soon ; and his conception, in this respect, is fantastic.
Plato betook himself for the bringing
in of righteousness to a visionary

republic in the clouds ; Isaiah,—and it
is the immortal glory of him and of his
race to have done so,—brought it in
upon earth.   But Immanuel and his
reign, for the eighth century before
Christ, were fantastic.   For the kingdom of Judah they were fantastic.
Immanuel and the remnant could not
come to reign under the conditions
there and then offered to them ; the
thing was impossible.

The reason of the impossibility is
quite simple.   The scale of things, in
petty States like Judah and Athens,
is too small; the numbers are too
scanty.   Admit that for the world, as
we hitherto know it, what the philosophers and prophets say is true :
that the majority are unsound.   Even

in communities with exceptional gifts, even in the Jewish State, the Athenian State, the majority are unsound.   But there is 'the remnant.'   Now the important thing, as regards States such as Judah and Athens, is not that the remnant bears but a small proportion to the majority; the remnant always bears a small proportion to the majority.   The grave thing for States like Judah and Athens is, that the remnant must in positive bulk be so small, and therefore so powerless for reform.   To be a voice outside the State, speaking to mankind or to the future, perhaps shaking the actual State to pieces in doing so, one man will suffice.   But to reform the State in order to save it, to preserve it by

changing it, a body of workers is
needed as well as a leader;—a considerable body of workers, placed at
many points, and operating in many
directions. This considerable body
of workers for good is what is wanting
in petty States such as were Athens
and Judah. It is said that the
Athenian State had in all but
350,000 inhabitants. It is calculated
that the population of the kingdom
of Judah did not exceed a million and
a quarter. The scale of things, I say,
is here too small, the numbers are too
scanty, to give us a remnant capable of
saving and perpetuating the community. The remnant, in these cases, may
influence the world and the future, may
transcend the State and survive it ; but

it cannot possibly transform the State
and perpetuate the State: for such
a work it is numerically too feeble.

Plato saw the impossibility. Isaiah
refused to accept it, but facts were too
strong for him. The Jewish State
could not be renewed and saved, and
he was wrong in thinking that it could.
And therefore I call his grand point
this other, where he was altogether
right: that the actual world of the
unsound majority, though it fancied
itself solid, and though most men
might call it solid, could not stand.
Let us read him again and again, until
we fix in our minds this true conviction of his, to edify us whenever we
see such a world existing: his indestructible conviction that such a world,

with its prosperities, idolatries, oppression, luxury, pleasures, drunkards,
careless women, governing classes,
systems of policy, strong alliances,
shall come to nought and pass away ;
that nothing can save it. Let us do
homage, also, to his indestructible
conviction that States are saved by
their righteous remnant, however
clearly we may at the same time
recognise that his own building on
this conviction was premature.

That, however, matters to us little.
For how different is the scale of
things in the modern States to which
we belong, how far greater are the
numbers ! It is impossible to overrate the importance of the new element
introduced into our calculations by

increasing the size of the remnant.
And in our great modern States,
where the scale of things is so large,
it does seem as if the remnant might
be so increased as to become an actual
power, even though the majority be
unsound.   Then the lover of wisdom
may come out from under his wall,
the lover of goodness will not be alone
among the wild beasts.   To enable the
remnant to succeed, a large strength-
ening of its numbers is everything.

Here is good hope for us, not only,
as for Plato's recluse, in departing
this life, but while we live and work
in it.   Only, before we dwell too
much on this hope, it is advisable to
make sure that we have earned the
right to entertain it.   We have earned

the right to entertain it, only when
we are at one with the philosophers
and prophets in their conviction re-
specting the world which now is, the
world of the unsound majority ; when
we feel what they mean, and when we
go thoroughly along with them in it.
Most of us, as I have said already, would
by no means have been with them when
they were here in life, and most of us
are not really with them now.   What
is saving ?   Our institutions, says an
American ; the British Constitution,
says an Englishman ; the civilising
mission of France, says a Frenchman.
But Plato and the sages, when they
are asked what is saving, answer :
' To love righteousness, and to be
convinced of the unprofitableness of

iniquity.' And Isaiah and the prophets, when they are asked the same
question, answer to just the same
effect : that what is saving is to 'order
one's conversation right'; to 'cease
to do evil'; to 'delight in the law of
the Eternal'; and to 'make one's
study in it all day long.'

The worst of it is, that this loving
of righteousness and this delighting
in the law of the Eternal sound rather
vague to us. Not that they are vague
really; indeed, they are less vague
than American institutions, or the
British Constitution, or the civilising
mission of France. But the phrases
sound vague because of the quantity
of matters they cover. The thing is
to have a brief but adequate enumera-

tion of these matters. The New Testament tells us how righteousness is composed. In England and America we have been brought up in familiarity with the New Testament. And so, before Mr. Bradlaugh on our side of the water, and the Congress of American Freethinkers on yours, banish it from our education and memory, let us take from the New Testament a text showing what it is that both Plato and the prophets mean when they tell us that we ought to love righteousness and to make our study in the law of the Eternal, but that the unsound majority do nothing of the kind. A score of texts offer themselves in a moment. Here is one which will serve very well :

'Whatsoever things are true, whatsoever things are elevated, whatsoever
things are just, whatsoever things are
pure, whatsoever things are amiable,
whatsoever things are of good report ;
if there be any virtue, and if there be
any praise ; have these in your mind,
let your thoughts run upon these.' [1]
That is what both Plato and the prophets mean by loving righteousness,
and making one's study in the law of
the Eternal.

Now the matters just enumerated
do not come much into the heads of
most of us, I suppose, when we are
thinking of politics. But the philosophers and prophets maintain that
these matters, and not those of which

[1] *Philippians*, iv. 8.

the heads of politicians are full, do
really govern politics and save
or destroy States. They save or
destroy them by a silent, inexorable
fatality; while the politicians are
making believe, plausibly and noisily,
with their American institutions,
British Constitution, and civilising
mission of France. And because
these matters are what do really
govern politics and save or destroy
States, Socrates maintained that in
his time he and a few philosophers,
who alone kept insisting on the good
of righteousness and the unprofitableness of iniquity, were the only real
politicians then living.

I say, if we are to derive comfort
from the doctrine of *the remnant* (and

there is great comfort to be derived from it), we must also hold fast to the austere but true doctrine as to what really governs politics, overrides with an inexorable fatality the combinations of the so-called politicians, and saves or destroys States. Having in mind things true, things elevated, things just, things pure, things amiable, things of good report; having these in mind, studying and loving these, is what saves States.

There is nothing like positive instances to illustrate general propositions of this kind, and to make them believed. I hesitate to take an instance from America. Possibly there are some people who think that already, on a former occasion, I have

said enough about America without
duly seeing and knowing it. So I
will take my instances from England,
and from England's neighbour and
old co-mate in history, France. The
instance from England I will take
first. I will take it from the grave
topic of England's relations with Ireland. I am not going to reproach
either England or Ireland. To reproach Ireland here would probably
be indiscreet. As to England, anything I may have to say against my
own countrymen I prefer to say at
home; America is the last place
where I should care to say it. However, I have no wish or intention now
to reproach either the English or the
Irish. But I want to show you from

D

England's relations with Ireland how right the philosophers and prophets are. Every one knows that there has been conquest and confiscation in Ireland. So there has elsewhere. Every one knows that the conquest and the confiscation have been attended with cupidity, oppression, and ill-usage. So they have elsewhere. 'Whatsoever things are just' are not exactly the study, so far as I know, of conquerors and confiscators anywhere; certainly they were not the study of the English conquerors of Ireland. A failure in justice is a source of danger to States. But it may be made up for and got over; it has been made up for and got over in many communities.

England's confiscations in Ireland are
a thing of the past; the penal laws
against Catholics are a thing of the
past; much has been done to make
up for the old failure in justice;
Englishmen generally think that it
has been pretty well made up for, and
that Irishmen ought to think so too.
And politicians invent Land Acts for
curing the last results of the old failure
in justice, for insuring the contentment
of the Irish with us, and for consoli-
dating the Union: and are surprised
and plaintive if it is not consolidated.
But now see how much more serious
people are the philosophers and prophets than the politicians. *Whatsoever things are amiable!*—the failure in
amiability, too, is a source of danger

and insecurity to States, as well as the failure in justice. And we English are not amiable, or at any rate, what in this case comes to the same thing, do not appear so. The politicians never thought of that! Quite outside their combinations lies this hindrance, tending to make their most elaborate combinations ineffectual. Thus the joint operation of two moral causes together, —the sort of causes which politicians do not seriously regard,—tells against the designs of the politicians with what seems to be an almost inexorable fatality. If there were not the failure in amiability, perhaps the original failure in justice might by this time have been got over; if there had not been the failure in justice, perhaps

the failure in amiability might not
have mattered much. The two failures together create a difficulty almost
insurmountable. Public men in England keep saying that it will be got
over. I hope that it will be got over,
and that the union between England
and Ireland may become as solid as
that between England and Scotland.
But it will not become solid by means
of the contrivances of the mere poli-
tician, or without the intervention of
moral causes of concord to heal the
mischief wrought by moral causes of
division. Everything, in this case,
depends upon the 'remnant,' its numbers and its powers of action.

My second instance is even more
important. It is so important, and its

reach is so wide, that I must go into it with some little fulness. The instance is taken from France. To France I have always felt myself powerfully drawn. People in England often accuse me of liking France and things French far too well. At all events I have paid special regard to them, and am always glad to confess how much I owe to them. M. Sainte-Beuve wrote to me in the last years of his life: 'You have passed through our life and literature by a deep inner line, which confers initiation, and which you will never lose.' *Vous avez traversé notre vie et notre littérature par une ligne intérieure, profonde, qui fait les initiés, et que vous ne perdrez jamais.* I wish I could think that this friendly testimony of that accomplished and charming man, one of my chief benefactors, were fully deserved. But I have pride and pleasure in quoting it; and I quote it to bear me out in saying, that whatever opinion I may express about France, I have at least been a not inattentive observer of that great country, and anything but a hostile one.

The question was once asked by the town clerk of Ephesus: 'What man is there that knoweth not how that the city of the Ephesians is a worshipper of the great goddess Diana?' Now really, when one looks at the popular literature of the French at this moment,—their popular novels, popular stage - plays, popular news-

papers,—and at the life of which this
literature of theirs is the index, one
is tempted to make a goddess out of
a word of their own, and then, like
the town clerk of Ephesus, to ask:
'What man is there that knoweth not
how that the city of the French is a
worshipper of the great goddess
Lubricity?' Or rather, as Greek is
the classic and euphonious language
for names of gods and goddesses, let
us take her name from the Greek
Testament, and call her the goddess
Aselgeia. That goddess has always
been a sufficient power amongst mankind, and her worship was generally
supposed to need restraining rather
than encouraging. But here is now a
whole popular literature, nay, and art

too, in France at her service! stimu-
lations and suggestions by her and to
her meet one in it at every turn. She
is becoming the great recognised
power there; never was anything like
it. M. Renan himself seems half
inclined to apologise for not having
paid her more attention. 'Nature
cares nothing for chastity,' says he;
Les frivoles ont peut-être raison;
'The gay people are perhaps in the
right.' Men even of this force salute
her; but the allegiance now paid to
her, in France, by the popular novel,
the popular newspaper, the popular
play, is, one may say, boundless.

I have no wish at all to preach to
the French; no intention whatever,
in what I now say, to upbraid or

wound them. I simply lay my finger on a fact in their present condition; a fact insufficiently noticed, as it seems to me, and yet extremely potent for mischief. It is well worth while to trace the manner of its growth and action.

The French have always had a leaning to the goddess of whom we speak, and have been willing enough to let the world know of their leaning, to pride themselves on their Gaulish salt, their gallantry, and so on. But things have come to their present head gradually. Catholicism was an obstacle; the serious element in the nation was another obstacle. But now just see the course which things have taken, and how they all, one may say,

have worked together for this goddess.
First, there was the original Gaul, the
basis of the French nation ; the Gaul,
gay, sociable, quick of sentiment,
quick of perception ; apt, however,
very apt, to be presumptuous and
puffed up. Then came the Roman
conquest, and from this we get a new
personage, the Gallo-Latin ; with the
Gaulish qualities for a basis, but with
Latin order, reason, lucidity, added,
and also Latin sensuality. Finally,
we have the Frankish conquest and
the Frenchman. The Frenchman
proper is the Gallo - Latin, with
Frankish or Germanic qualities added
and infused. No mixture could be
better. The Germans have plenty of
faults, but in this combination they

seem not to have taken hold; the
Germans seem to have given of their
seriousness and honesty to the con-
quered Gallo-Latin, and not of their
brutality. And mediæval France,
which exhibits the combination and
balance, under the influence then
exercised by Catholicism, of Gaulish
quickness and gaiety with Latin
rationality and German seriousness,
offers to our view the soundest and
the most attractive stage, perhaps, in
all French history.

But the balance could not be maintained; at any rate, it was not maintained. Mediæval Catholicism lost
its virtue. The serious Germanic
races made the Reformation, feeling
that without it there was no safety

and continuance for those moral ideas
which they loved and which were the
ground of their being.   France did
not go with the Reformation; the
Germanic qualities in her were not
strong enough to make her go with
it.   'France did not want a reformation which was a moral one,' is
Michelet's account of the matter :
*La France ne voulait pas de réforme
morale.*   Let us put the case more
favourably for her, and say that perhaps, with her quick perception,
France caught sense, from the very
outset, of that intellectual unsoundness and incompleteness in the Reformation, which is now so visible.   But,
at any rate, the Reformation did not
carry France with it; and the Ger-

manic side in the Frenchman, his
Germanic qualities, thus received a
check. They subsisted, however, in
good force still; the new knowledge
and new ideas, brought by the re-
vival of letters, gave an animating
stimulus; and in the seventeenth
century the Gaulish gaiety and quickness of France, the Latin rationality,
and the still subsisting German seriousness, all combining under the
puissant breath of the Renascence,
produced a literature, the strongest,
the most substantial and the most
serious which the French have ever
succeeded in producing, and which
has, indeed, consummate and splendid
excellences.

Still, the Germanic side in the

Frenchman had received a check, and in the next century this side became quite attenuated. The Germanic steadiness and seriousness gave way more and more ; the Gaulish salt, the Gaulish gaiety, quickness, sentiment, and sociability, the Latin rationality, prevailed more and more, and had the field nearly to themselves. They produced a brilliant and most efficacious literature,—the French literature of the eighteenth century. The goddess Aselgeia had her part in it ; it was a literature to be praised with reserves ; it was, above all, a revolutionary literature. But European institutions were then in such a superannuated condition, straightforward and just perception, free thought and rationality, were at such a discount, that the brilliant French literature in which these qualities predominated, and which by their predominance was made revolutionary, had in the eighteenth century a great mission to fulfil, and fulfilled it victoriously.

The mission is fulfilled, but meanwhile the Germanic quality in the Frenchman seems pretty nearly to have died out, and the Gallo-Latin in him has quite got the upper hand. Of course there are individuals and groups who are to be excepted; I will allow any number of exceptions you please; and in the mass of the French people, which works and is silent, there may be treasures of

resource. But taking the Frenchman
who is commonly in view—the usual
type of speaking, doing, vocal, visible
Frenchman—we may say, and he will
probably be not at all displeased at
our saying, that the German in him
has nearly died out, and the Gallo-
Latin has quite got the upper hand.
For us, however, this means that the
chief source of seriousness and of
moral ideas is failing and drying up
in him, and that what remains are the
sources of Gaulish salt, and quickness,
and sentiment, and sociability, and
sensuality, and rationality. And, of
course, the play and working of these
qualities is altered by their being no
longer in combination with a dose of
German seriousness, but left to work

E

by themselves. Left to work by themselves, they give us what we call the *homme sensuel moyen*, the average sensual man. The highest art, the art which by its height, depth, and gravity possesses religiousness,— such as the Greeks had, the art of Pindar and Phidias; such as the Italians had, the art of Dante and Michael Angelo,—this art, with the training which it gives and the standard which it sets up, the French have never had. On the other hand, they had a dose of German seriousness, a Germanic bent for ideas of moral duty, which neither the Greeks had, nor the Italians. But if this dies out, what is left is the *homme sensuel moyen*. This average sensual man

has his very advantageous qualities.
He has his gaiety, quickness, sentiment, sociability, rationality.   He has
his horror of sour strictness, false
restraint, hypocrisy, obscurantism,
cretinism, and the rest of it.   And
this is very well ; but on the serious,
moral side he is almost ludicrously
insufficient.   Fine sentiments about
his dignity and his honour and his
heart, about the dignity and the
honour and the heart of France, and
his adoration of her, do duty for him
here ; grandiose phrases about the
spectacle offered in France and in the
French Republic of the ideal for our
race, of the *épanouissement de l'élite
de l'humanité*, 'the coming into blow
of the choice flower of humanity.'   In

M. Victor Hugo we have (his worshippers must forgive me for saying
so) the average sensual man impassioned and grandiloquent ; in M. Zola
we have the average sensual man going near the ground. ' Happy the
son,' cries M. Victor Hugo, ' of whom
one can say, " He has consoled his
mother ! " Happy the poet of whom
one can say, " He has consoled his
country ! " ' The French themselves,
even when they are severest, call this
kind of thing by only the mild name
of emphasis, '*emphase*,'—other people
call it fustian. And a surly Johnson
will growl out in answer, at one time,
that ' Patriotism is the last refuge of a
scoundrel ' ; at another time, that fine
sentiments about *ma mère* are the last

refuge of a scoundrel.   But what they
really are is the creed which in France
the average sensual man rehearses,
to do duty for serious moral ideas.
And, as the result, we have a popular
literature and a popular art serving,
as has been already said, the goddess
Aselgeia.

Such an art and literature easily
make their way everywhere.   In
England and America the French
literature of the seventeenth century
is peculiarly fitted to do great good,
and nothing but good; it can hardly
be too much studied by us.   And it is
studied by us very little.   The French
literature of the eighteenth century,
also, has qualities to do us much
good, and we are not likely to take

harm from its other qualities; we
may study it to our great profit and
advantage. And it is studied by us
very little. The higher French literature of the present day has more
knowledge and a wider range than
its great predecessors, but less soundness and perfection, and it exerts
much less influence than they did.
Action and influence are now with
the lower literature of France, with
the popular literature in the service
of the goddess Aselgeia. And this
popular modern French literature,
and the art which corresponds to it,
bid fair to make their way in England
and America far better than their predecessors. They appeal to instincts
so universal and accessible; they

appeal, people are beginning boldly
to say, to Nature herself. Few things
have lately struck me more than M.
Renan's dictum, which I have already
quoted, about what used to be called
the virtue of chastity. The dictum
occurs in his very interesting auto-
biography, published but the other
day. M. Renan, whose genius I un-
feignedly admire, is, I need hardly
say, a man of the most perfect pro-
priety of life ; he has told us so himself. He was brought up for a priest,
and he thinks it would not have been
in good taste for him to become a free
liver. But this abstinence is a mere
matter of personal delicacy, a display
of good and correct taste on his own
part in his own very special circum-

stances. 'Nature,' he cries, 'cares
nothing about chastity.' What a slap
in the face to the sticklers for 'Whatsoever things are pure'!

I have had to take a long sweep to
arrive at the point which I wished to
reach. If we are to enjoy the benefit,
I said, of the comfortable doctrine of
the remnant, we must be capable of
receiving also, and of holding fast,
the hard doctrine of the unsoundness
of the majority, and of the certainty
that the unsoundness of the majority,
if it is not withstood and remedied,
must be their ruin. And therefore,
even though a gifted man like M.
Renan may be so carried away by
the tide of opinion in France where
he lives, as to say that Nature cares

nothing about chastity, and to see with
amused indulgence the worship of the
great goddess Lubricity, let us stand
fast, and say that her worship is against
nature, human nature, and that it is
ruin. For this is the test of its being
against human nature, that for human
societies it is ruin. And the test is
one from which there is no escape, as
from the old tests in such matters
there may be. For if you allege that
it is the will of God that we should
be pure, the sceptical Gallo-Latins
will tell you that they do not know
any such person. And in like manner, if it is said that those who serve
the goddess Aselgeia shall not inherit
the kingdom of God, the Gallo-Latin
may tell you that he does not believe

in any such place. But that the sure
tendency and upshot of things estab-
lishes that the service of the goddess
Aselgeia is ruin, that her followers are
marred and stunted by it and disquali-
fied for the ideal society of the future,
is an infallible test to employ.

The saints admonish us to let our
thoughts run upon whatsoever things
are pure, if we would inherit the kingdom of God; and the divine Plato
tells us that we have within us a
many-headed beast and a man, and
that by dissoluteness we feed and
strengthen the beast in us, and starve
the man; and finally, following the
divine Plato among the sages at a
humble distance, comes the prosaic
and unfashionable Paley, and says in

his precise way that 'this vice has a
tendency, which other species of vice
have not so directly, to unsettle and
weaken the powers of the understand-
ing; as well as, I think, in a greater
degree than other vices, to render
the heart thoroughly corrupt.'   True;
and once admitted and fostered, it
eats like a canker, and with difficulty
can ever be brought to let go its hold
again, but for ever tightens it.   Hardness and insolence come in its train;
an insolence which grows until it ends
by exasperating and alienating everybody; a hardness which grows until
the man can at last scarcely take
pleasure in anything, outside the service of his goddess, except cupidity
and greed, and cannot be touched

with emotion by any language except fustian. Such are the fruits of the worship of the great goddess Aselgeia.

So, instead of saying that Nature cares nothing about chastity, let us say that human nature, *our* nature, cares about it a great deal. Let us say that, by her present popular literature, France gives proof that she is suffering from a dangerous and perhaps fatal disease ; and that it is not clericalism which is the real enemy to the French so much as their goddess ; and if they can none of them see this themselves, it is only a sign of how far the disease has gone, and the case is so much the worse. The case is so much the worse ; and for men in such case to be so vehemently

busy about clerical and dynastic in-
trigues at home, and about alliances
and colonial acquisitions and purifica-
tions of the flag abroad, might well
make one borrow of the prophets and
exclaim, 'Surely ye are perverse'!
perverse to neglect your really press-
ing matters for those secondary ones.
And when the ingenious and inex-
haustible M. Blowitz, of our great
London *Times*, who sees everybody
and knows everything, when he ex-
pounds the springs of politics and
the causes of the fall and success
of ministries, and the combinations
which have not been tried but should
be, and takes upon him the mystery
of things in the way with which we
are so familiar, — to this wise man

himself one is often tempted, again,
to say with the prophets : ' Yet the
Eternal also is wise, and will not call
back his words.'   M. Blowitz is not
the only wise one ; the Eternal has
his wisdom also, and somehow or
other it is always the Eternal's wisdom which at last carries the day.
The Eternal has attached to certain
moral causes the safety or the ruin of
States, and the present popular literature of France is a sign that she has
a most dangerous moral disease.

Now if the disease goes on and
increases, then, whatever sagacious
advice M. Blowitz may give, and
whatever political combinations may
be tried, and whether France gets
colonies or not, and whether she allies

herself with this nation or with that, things will only go from bad to worse with her; she will more and more lose her powers of soul and spirit, her intellectual productiveness, her skill in counsel, her might for war, her formidableness as a foe, her value as an ally, and the life of that famous State will be more and more impaired, until it perish. And this is that hard but true doctrine of the sages and prophets, of the inexorable fatality of operation, in moral failure of the unsound majority, to impair and destroy States. But we will not talk or think of destruction for a State with such gifts and graces as France, and which has had such a place in history, and to which we, many of us, owe so much delight and so much

good.   And yet if France had no
greater numbers than the Athens of
Plato or the Judah of Isaiah, I do not
see how she could well escape out of
the throttling arms of her goddess and
recover.   She must recover through
a powerful and profound renewal, a
great inward change, brought about
by 'the remnant' amongst her people ;
and, for this, a remnant small in numbers would not suffice.   But in a
France of thirty-five millions, who
shall set bounds to the numbers of
the remnant, or to its effectualness
and power of victory ?

In these United States (for I come
round to the United States at last)
. you are fifty millions and more.   I
suppose that, as in England, as in

France, as everywhere, so likewise
here, the majority of people doubt
very much whether the majority is
unsound; or, rather, they have no
doubt at all about the matter, they are
sure that it is not unsound. But let
us consent to-night to remain to the
end in the ideas of the sages and prophets whom we have been following
all along; and let us suppose that in
the present actual stage of the world,
as in all the stages through which the
world has passed hitherto, the majority
is and must be in general unsound
everywhere, — even in the United
States, even here in New York itself.
Where is the failure ? I have already,
in the past, speculated in the abstract
about you, perhaps, too much. But I

F

suppose that in a democratic community like this, with its newness, its magni-
tude its strength, its life of business, its
sheer freedom and equality, the danger
is in the absence of the discipline of
respect; in hardness and materialism,
exaggeration and boastfulness; in a
false smartness, a false audacity, a
want of soul and delicacy. 'Whatsoever things are *elevated*,'—whatsoever
things are nobly serious, have true
elevation,[1]—that perhaps, in our cata-
logue of maxims which are to possess
the mind, is the maxim which points
to where the failure of the unsound
majority, in a great democracy like
yours, will probably lie. At any rate
let us for the moment agree to sup-

[1] Ὅσα σεμνά.

pose so. And the philosophers and the prophets, whom I at any rate am disposed to believe, and who say that moral causes govern the standing and the falling of States, will tell us that the failure to mind whatsoever things are elevated must impair with an inexorable fatality the life of a nation, just as the failure to mind whatsoever things are just, or whatsoever things are amiable, or whatsoever things are pure, will impair it; and that if the failure to mind whatsoever things are elevated should be real in your American democracy, and should grow into a disease, and take firm hold on you, then the life of even these great United States must inevitably suffer and be impaired more and more, until it perish.

Then from this hard doctrine we will betake ourselves to the more comfortable doctrine of *the remnant*. 'The remnant shall return;' shall 'convert and be healed' itself first, and shall then recover the unsound majority. And you are fifty millions and growing apace. What a remnant yours may be, surely! A remnant of how great numbers, how mighty strength, how irresistible efficacy! Yet we must not go too fast, either, nor make too sure of our efficacious remnant. Mere multitude will not give us a saving remnant with certainty. The Assyrian Empire had multitude, the Roman Empire had multitude; yet neither the one nor the other could produce a sufficing remnant any more than Athens or Judah could produce it, and both Assyria and Rome perished like Athens and Judah.

But you are something more than a people of fifty millions. You are fifty millions mainly sprung, as we in England are mainly sprung, from that German stock which has faults indeed, —faults which have diminished the extent of its influence, diminished its power of attraction and the interest of its history, and which seems moreover just now, from all I can see and hear, to be passing through a not very happy moment, morally, in Germany proper. Yet of the German stock it is, I think, true, as my father said more than fifty years ago, that it has

been a stock ' of the most moral races
of men that the world has yet seen,
with the soundest laws, the least
violent passions, the fairest domestic
and civil virtues.' You come, therefore, of about the best parentage which
a modern nation can have. Then
you have had, as we in England have
also had, but more entirely than we
and more exclusively, the Puritan
discipline. Certainly I am not blind
to the faults of that discipline. Certainly I do not wish it to remain in
possession of the field for ever, or too
long. But as a stage and a discipline,
and as means for enabling that poor
inattentive and immoral creature, man,
to love and appropriate and make part
of his being divine ideas, on which he

could not otherwise have laid or kept
hold, the discipline of Puritanism has
been invaluable ; and the more I read
history, the more I see of mankind,
the more I recognise its value.   Well,
then, you are not merely a multitude
of fifty millions ; you are fifty millions
sprung from this excellent Germanic
stock, having passed through this
excellent Puritan discipline, and set in
this enviable and unbounded country.
Even supposing, therefore, that by the
necessity of things your majority must
in the present stage of the world probably be unsound, what a remnant, I
say,—what an incomparable, all-trans-
forming remnant,—you may fairly
hope with your numbers, if things go
happily, to have!

LITERATURE AND SCIENCE

PRACTICAL people talk with a smile
of Plato and of his absolute ideas;
and it is impossible to deny that
Plato's ideas do often seem unprac-
tical and impracticable, and especially
when one views them in connexion
with the life of a great work-a-day
world like the United States. The
necessary staple of the life of such a
world Plato regards with disdain;
handicraft and trade and the working professions he regards with dis-

dain ; but what becomes of the life
of an industrial modern community
if you take handicraft and trade and
the working professions out of it ?
The base mechanic arts and handi-
crafts, says Plato, bring about a
natural weakness in the principle of
excellence in a man, so that he cannot govern the ignoble growths in
him, but nurses them, and cannot
understand fostering any other. Those
who exercise such arts and trades, as
they have their bodies, he says, marred
by their vulgar businesses, so they
have their souls, too, bowed and
broken by them. And if one of
these uncomely people has a mind to
seek self-culture and philosophy, Plato
compares him to a bald little tinker,

who has scraped together money, and
has got his release from service, and
has had a bath, and bought a new
coat, and is rigged out like a bride-
groom about to marry the daughter
of his master who has fallen into poor
and helpless estate.

Nor do the working professions fare
any better than trade at the hands of
Plato.   He draws for us an inimitable
picture of the working lawyer, and of
his life of bondage ; he shows how this
bondage from his youth up has stunted
and warped him, and made him small
and crooked of soul, encompassing him
with difficulties which he is not man
enough to rely on justice and truth as
means to encounter, but has recourse,
for help out of them, to falsehood and

wrong. And so, says Plato, this poor
creature is bent and broken, and grows
up from boy to man without a particle
of soundness in him, although exceed-
ingly smart and clever in his own
esteem.

One cannot refuse to admire the
artist who draws these pictures. But
we say to ourselves that his ideas
show the influence of a primitive and
obsolete order of things, when the
warrior caste and the priestly caste
were alone in honour, and the humble
work of the world was done by slaves.
We have now changed all that; the
modern majority consists in work, as
Emerson declares; and in work, we
may add, principally of such plain and
dusty kind as the work of cultivators

of the ground, handicraftsmen, men of trade and business, men of the working professions. Above all is this true in a great industrious community such as that of the United States.

Now education, many people go on to say, is still mainly governed by the ideas of men like Plato, who lived when the warrior caste and the priestly or philosophical class were alone in honour, and the really useful part of the community were slaves. It is an education fitted for persons of leisure in such a community. This education passed from Greece and Rome to the feudal communities of Europe, where also the warrior caste and the priestly caste were alone held in honour, and where the really useful and working part of the community, though not nominally slaves as in the pagan world, were practically not much better off than slaves, and not more seriously regarded. And how absurd it is, people end by saying, to inflict this education upon an industrious modern community, where very few indeed are persons of leisure, and the mass to be considered has not leisure, but is bound, for its own great good, and for the great good of the world at large, to plain labour and to industrial pursuits, and the education in question tends necessarily to make men dissatisfied with these pursuits and unfitted for them!

That is what is said. So far I must defend Plato, as to plead that his view of education and studies is in the general, as it seems to me, sound enough, and fitted for all sorts and conditions of men, whatever their pursuits may be. 'An intelligent man,' says Plato, 'will prize those studies which result in his soul getting soberness, righteousness, and wisdom, and will less value the others.' I cannot consider *that* a bad description of the aim of education, and of the motives which should govern us in the choice of studies, whether we are preparing ourselves for a hereditary seat in the English House of Lords or for the pork trade in Chicago.

Still I admit that Plato's world was not ours, that his scorn of trade and handicraft is fantastic, that he had no

conception of a great industrial community such as that of the United States,
and that such a community must and
will shape its education to suit its own
needs.   If the usual education handed
down to it from the past does not suit
it, it will certainly before long drop
this and try another.   The usual education in the past has been mainly
literary.   The question is whether the
studies which were long supposed to
be the best for all of us are practically
the best now ; whether others are not
better.   The tyranny of the past,
many think, weighs on us injuriously
in the predominance given to letters
in education.   The question is raised
whether, to meet the needs of our
modern life, the predominance ought

not now to pass from letters to science;
and naturally the question is nowhere
raised with more energy than here in
the United States. The design of
abasing what is called 'mere literary
instruction and education,' and of ex-
alting what is called 'sound, extensive,
and practical scientific knowledge,'
is, in this intensely modern world of
the United States, even more perhaps
than in Europe, a very popular design,
and makes great and rapid progress.

I am going to ask whether the
present movement for ousting letters
from their old predominance in education, and for transferring the predominance in education to the natural
sciences, whether this brisk and
flourishing movement ought to pre-

vail, and whether it is likely that in
the end it really will prevail. An
objection may be raised which I will
anticipate. My own studies have
been almost wholly in letters, and my
visits to the field of the natural
sciences have been very slight and
inadequate, although those sciences
have always strongly moved my
curiosity. A man of letters, it will
perhaps be said, is not competent
to discuss the comparative merits of
letters and natural science as means
of education. To this objection I
reply, first of all, that his incompet-
ence, if he attempts the discussion but is really incompetent for it,
will be abundantly visible; nobody
will be taken in; he will have plenty

G

of sharp observers and critics to save
mankind from that danger. But the
line I am going to follow is, as you
will soon discover, so extremely simple,
that perhaps it may be followed without failure even by one who for a more
ambitious line of discussion would be
quite incompetent.

Some of you may possibly remem-
ber a phrase of mine which has been
the object of a good deal of comment ;
an observation to the effect that in
our culture, the aim being *to know
ourselves and the world*, we have, as
the means to this end, *to know the
best which has been thought and said
in the world*. A man of science, who
is also an excellent writer and the
very prince of debaters, Professor

Huxley, in a discourse at the opening of Sir Josiah Mason's college at Birmingham, laying hold of this phrase, expanded it by quoting some more words of mine, which are these : ' The civilised world is to be regarded as now being, for intellectual and spiritual purposes, one great confederation, bound to a joint action and working to a common result ; and whose members have for their proper outfit a knowledge of Greek, Roman, and Eastern antiquity, and of one another. Special local and temporary advantages being put out of account, that modern nation will in the intellectual and spiritual sphere make most progress, which most thoroughly carries out this programme.'

Now on my phrase, thus enlarged, Professor Huxley remarks that when I speak of the above-mentioned knowledge as enabling us to know ourselves and the world, I assert *literature* to contain the materials which suffice for thus making us know ourselves and the world. But it is not by any means clear, says he, that after having learnt all which ancient and modern literatures have to tell us, we have laid a sufficiently broad and deep foundation for that criticism of life, that knowledge of ourselves and the world, which constitutes culture. On the contrary, Professor Huxley declares that he finds himself 'wholly unable to admit that either nations or individuals will really

advance, if their outfit draws nothing
from the stores of physical science.
An army without weapons of pre-
cision, and with no particular base of
operations, might more hopefully
enter upon a campaign on the Rhine,
than a man, devoid of a knowledge
of what physical science has done in
the last century, upon a criticism of
life.'

This shows how needful it is for
those who are to discuss any matter
together, to have a common under-
standing as to the sense of the terms
they employ,—how needful, and how
difficult. What Professor Huxley
says, implies just the reproach which
is so often brought against the study
of *belles lettres*, as they are called :

that the study is an elegant one, but
slight and ineffectual; a smattering
of Greek and Latin and other orna-
mental things, of little use for any
one whose object is to get at truth,
and to be a practical man. So, too,
M. Renan talks of the 'superficial
humanism' of a school-course which
treats us as if we were all going to
be poets, writers, preachers, orators,
and he opposes this humanism to
positive science, or the critical search
after truth. And there is always a
tendency in those who are remon-
strating against the predominance of
letters in education, to understand by
letters *belles lettres*, and by *belles lettres*
a superficial humanism, the opposite
of science or true knowledge.

But when we talk of knowing Greek and Roman antiquity, for instance, which is the knowledge people have called the humanities, I for my part mean a knowledge which is something more than a superficial humanism, mainly decorative. 'I call all teaching *scientific*,' says Wolf, the critic of Homer, 'which is systematically laid out and followed up to its original sources. For example : a knowledge of classical antiquity is scientific when the remains of classical antiquity are correctly studied in the original languages.' There can be no doubt that Wolf is perfectly right; that all learning is scientific which is systematically laid out and followed up to its original sources, and that a genuine humanism is scientific.

When I speak of knowing Greek and Roman antiquity, therefore, as a help to knowing ourselves and the world, I mean more than a knowledge of so much vocabulary, so much grammar, so many portions of authors in the Greek and Latin languages, I mean knowing the Greeks and Romans, and their life and genius, and what they were and did in the world; what we get from them, and what is its value. That, at least, is the ideal; and when we talk of endeavouring to know Greek and Roman antiquity, as a help to knowing ourselves and the world, we mean endeavouring so to know them as to satisfy this ideal, however much we may still fall short of it.

The same also as to knowing our own and other modern nations, with the like aim of getting to understand ourselves and the world. To know the best that has been thought and said by the modern nations, is to know, says Professor Huxley, 'only what modern *literatures* have to tell us; it is the criticism of life contained in modern literature.' And yet 'the distinctive character of our times,' he urges, 'lies in the vast and constantly increasing part which is played by natural knowledge.' And how, therefore, can a man, devoid of knowledge of what physical science has done in the last century, enter hopefully upon a criticism of modern life ?

Let us, I say, be agreed about the meaning of the terms we are using. I talk of knowing the best which has been thought and uttered in the world ; Professor Huxley says this means knowing *literature*. Literature is a large word ; it may mean everything written with letters or printed in a book. Euclid's *Elements* and Newton's *Principia* are thus literature. All knowledge that reaches us through books is literature. But by literature Professor Huxley means *belles lettres*. He means to make me say, that knowing the best which has been thought and said by the modern nations is knowing their *belles lettres* and no more. And this is no sufficient equipment, he argues, for a criticism of modern life. But as I do not mean, by knowing ancient Rome, knowing merely more or less of Latin *belles lettres*, and taking no account of Rome's military, and political, and legal, and administrative work in the world; and as, by knowing ancient Greece, I understand knowing her as the giver of Greek art, and the guide to a free and right use of reason and to scientific method, and the founder of our mathematics and physics and astronomy and biology, —I understand knowing her as all this, and not merely knowing certain Greek poems, and histories, and treatises, and speeches,—so as to the know-

ledge of modern nations also.   By
knowing modern nations, I mean not
merely knowing their *belles lettres*, but
knowing also what has been done by
such men as Copernicus, Galileo, Newton, Darwin.   'Our ancestors learned,'
says Professor Huxley, 'that the earth
is the centre of the visible universe,
and that man is the cynosure of
things terrestrial; and more especially was it inculcated that the course
of nature had no fixed order, but
that it could be, and constantly
was, altered.'   But for us now, con-
tinues Professor Huxley, 'the notions
of the beginning and the end of the
world entertained by our forefathers
are no longer credible.   It is very
certain that the earth is not the chief

body in the material universe, and
that the world is not subordinated
to man's use.   It is even more certain
that nature is the expression of a
definite order, with which nothing
interferes.'   'And yet,' he cries,
'the purely classical education advo-
cated by the representatives of the
humanists in our day gives no inkling
of all this!'

In due place and time I will just
touch upon that vexed question of
classical education; but at present
the question is as to what is meant
by knowing the best which modern
nations have thought and said.   It
is not knowing their *belles lettres*
merely which is meant.   To know
Italian *belles lettres* is not to know

Italy, and to know English *belles lettres* is not to know England. Into knowing Italy and England there comes a great deal more, Galileo and Newton amongst it. The reproach of being a superficial humanism, a tincture of *belles lettres*, may attach rightly enough to some other disciplines; but to the particular discipline recommended when I proposed knowing the best that has been thought and said in the world, it does not apply. In that best I certainly include what in modern times has been thought and said by the great observers and knowers of nature.

There is, therefore, really no question between Professor Huxley and

me as to whether knowing the great
results of the modern scientific study
of nature is not required as a part of
our culture, as well as knowing the
products of literature and art. But
to follow the processes by which those
results are reached, ought, say the
friends of physical science, to be made
the staple of education for the bulk of
mankind. And here there does arise
a question between those whom Professor Huxley calls with playful sar-
casm 'the Levites of culture,' and
those whom the poor humanist is
sometimes apt to regard as its Ne-
buchadnezzars.

The great results of the scientific
investigation of nature we are agreed
upon knowing, but how much of our

study are we bound to give to the processes by which those results are reached? The results have their visible bearing on human life. But all the processes, too, all the items of fact, by which those results are reached and established, are interesting. All knowledge is interesting to a wise man, and the knowledge of nature is interesting to all men. It is very interesting to know, that, from the albuminous white of the egg, the chick in the egg gets the materials for its flesh, bones, blood, and feathers; while, from the fatty yolk of the egg, it gets the heat and energy which enable it at length to break its shell and begin the world. It is less interesting, perhaps, but still it is interesting, to know that when a taper burns, the wax is converted into carbonic acid and water. Moreover, it is quite true that the habit of deal-ing with facts, which is given by the study of nature, is, as the friends of physical science praise it for being, an excellent discipline. The appeal, in the study of nature, is constantly to observation and experiment; not only is it said that the thing is so, but we can be made to see that it is so. Not only does a man tell us that when a taper burns the wax is converted into carbonic acid and water, as a man may tell us, if he likes, that Charon is punting his ferry-boat on the river Styx, or that Victor Hugo is a sublime poet, or Mr. Gladstone the most ad-

mirable of statesmen ; but we are
made to see that the conversion into
carbonic acid and water does actually
happen.   This reality of natural knowledge it is, which makes the friends of
physical science contrast it, as a knowledge of things, with the humanist's
knowledge, which is, say they, a
knowledge of words.   And hence
Professor Huxley is moved to lay it
down that, 'for the purpose of attain-
ing real culture, an exclusively scientific education is at least as effectual
as an exclusively literary education.'
And a certain President of the Section
for Mechanical Science in the British
Association is, in Scripture phrase,
'very bold,' and declares that if a
man, in his mental training, 'has sub-

stituted literature and history for
natural science, he has chosen the
less useful alternative.' But whether
we go these lengths or not, we must
all admit that in natural science the
habit gained of dealing with facts is
a most valuable discipline, and that
every one should have some experience of it.

More than this, however, is de-
manded by the reformers. It is proposed to make the training in natural
science the main part of education,
for the great majority of mankind at
any rate. And here, I confess, I part
company with the friends of physical
science, with whom up to this point
I have been agreeing. In differing
from them, however, I wish to pro-

ceed with the utmost caution and diffidence. The smallness of my own acquaintance with the disciplines of natural science is ever before my mind, and I am fearful of doing these disciplines an injustice. The ability and pugnacity of the partisans of natural science make them formidable persons to contradict. The tone of tentative inquiry, which befits a being of dim faculties and bounded knowledge, is the tone I would wish to take and not to depart from. At present it seems to me, that those who are for giving to natural knowledge, as they call it, the chief place in the education of the majority of mankind, leave one important thing out of their account : the constitution of human nature. But I put this forward on the strength of some facts not at all recondite, very far from it ; facts capable of being stated in the simplest possible fashion, and to which, if I so state them, the man of science will, I am sure, be willing to allow their due weight.

Deny the facts altogether, I think, he hardly can. He can hardly deny, that when we set ourselves to enumerate the powers which go to the building up of human life, and say that they are the power of conduct, the power of intellect and knowledge, the power of beauty, and the power of social life and manners,—he can hardly deny that this scheme, though drawn in rough and plain lines enough, and

not pretending to scientific exactness,
does yet give a fairly true representa-
tion of the matter. Human nature is
built up by these powers; we have
the need for them all. When we
have rightly met and adjusted the
claims of them all, we shall then be in
a fair way for getting soberness and
righteousness, with wisdom. This is
evident enough, and the friends of
physical science would admit it.

But perhaps they may not have
sufficiently observed another thing:
namely, that the several powers just
mentioned are not isolated, but there
is, in the generality of mankind, a
perpetual tendency to relate them one
to another in divers ways. With one
such way of relating them I am parti-

cularly concerned now. Following our instinct for intellect and knowledge, we acquire pieces of knowledge; and presently, in the generality of men, there arises the desire to relate these pieces of knowledge to our sense for conduct, to our sense for beauty,—and there is weariness and dissatisfaction if the desire is baulked. Now in this desire lies, I think, the strength of that hold which letters have upon us.

All knowledge is, as I said just now, interesting; and even items of knowledge which from the nature of the case cannot well be related, but must stand isolated in our thoughts, have their interest. Even lists of exceptions have their interest. If we

are studying Greek accents, it is interesting to know that *pais* and *pas*, and
some other monosyllables of the same
form of declension, do not take the
circumflex upon the last syllable of
the genitive plural, but vary, in this
respect, from the common rule.   If we
are studying physiology, it is interesting to know that the pulmonary artery
carries dark blood and the pulmonary
vein carries bright blood, departing in
this respect from the common rule for
the division of labour between the
veins and the arteries.   But every
one knows how we seek naturally to
combine the pieces of our knowledge
together, to bring them under general
rules, to relate them to principles ;
and how unsatisfactory and tiresome it

would be to go on for ever learning lists of exceptions, or accumulating items of fact which must stand isolated.

Well, that same need of relating our knowledge, which operates here within the sphere of our knowledge itself, we shall find operating, also, outside that sphere. We experience, as we go on learning and knowing,— the vast majority of us experience,— the need of relating what we have learnt and known to the sense which we have in us for conduct, to the sense which we have in us for beauty.

A certain Greek prophetess of Mantineia in Arcadia, Diotima by name, once explained to the philosopher Socrates that love, and impulse, and bent of all kinds, is, in fact, nothing else but the desire in men that good should for ever be present to them. This desire for good, Diotima assured Socrates, is our fundamental desire, of which fundamental desire every impulse in us is only some one particular form. And therefore this fundamental desire it is, I suppose, —this desire in men that good should be for ever present to them,—which acts in us when we feel the impulse for relating our knowledge to our sense for conduct and to our sense for beauty. At any rate, with men in general the instinct exists. Such is human nature. And the instinct, it will be admitted, is innocent, and human nature is preserved by our following the lead of its innocent in-

stincts.   Therefore, in seeking to
gratify this instinct in question, we
are following the instinct of self-preservation in humanity.

But, no doubt, some kinds of knowledge cannot be made to directly serve
the instinct in question, cannot be
directly related to the sense for
beauty, to the sense for conduct.
These are instrument-knowledges ;
they lead on to other knowledges,
which can.   A man who passes his
life in instrument-knowledges is a
specialist.   They may be invaluable
as instruments to something beyond,
for those who have the gift thus to
employ them ; and they may be disciplines in themselves wherein it is
useful for every one to have some

schooling. But it is inconceivable
that the generality of men should pass
all their mental life with Greek accents
or with formal logic. My friend Professor Sylvester, who is one of the
first mathematicians in the world,
holds transcendental doctrines as to
the virtue of mathematics, but those
doctrines are not for common men.
In the very Senate House and heart
of our English Cambridge I once ven-
tured, though not without an apology
for my profaneness, to hazard the
opinion that for the majority of mankind a little of mathematics, even,
goes a long way. Of course this is
quite consistent with their being of
immense importance as an instrument
to something else; but it is the few

who have the aptitude for thus using them, not the bulk of mankind.

The natural sciences do not, however, stand on the same footing with these instrument - knowledges. Experience shows us that the generality of men will find more interest in learning that, when a taper burns, the wax is converted into carbonic acid and water, or in learning the explanation of the phenomenon of dew, or in learning how the circulation of the blood is carried on, than they find in learning that the genitive plural of *pais* and *pas* does not take the circumflex on the termination. And one piece of natural knowledge is added to another, and others are added to that, and at last we come to proposi-

tions so interesting as Mr. Darwin's
famous proposition that 'our ancestor
was a hairy quadruped furnished with
a tail and pointed ears, probably arboreal in his habits.'   Or we come to
propositions of such reach and magni-
tude as those which Professor Huxley
delivers, when he says that the notions
of our forefathers about the beginning
and the end of the world were all
wrong, and that nature is the expression of a definite order with which
nothing interferes.

Interesting, indeed, these results of
science are, important they are, and
we should all of us be acquainted with
them.   But what I now wish you to
mark is, that we are still, when they
are propounded to us and we receive

them, we are still in the sphere of
intellect and knowledge.   And for the
generality of men there will be found,
I say, to arise, when they have duly
taken in the proposition that their
ancestor was 'a hairy quadruped furnished with a tail and pointed ears,
probably arboreal in his habits,' there
will be found to arise an invincible
desire to relate this proposition to the
sense in us for conduct, and to the
sense in us for beauty.   But this the
men of science will not do for us, and
will hardly even profess to do.   They
will give us other pieces of knowledge,
other facts, about other animals and
their ancestors, or about plants, or
about stones, or about stars ; and they
may finally bring us to those great

'general conceptions of the universe,
which are forced upon us all,' says
Professor Huxley, 'by the progress
of physical science.' But still it will
be *knowledge* only which they give
us; knowledge not put for us into
relation with our sense for conduct,
our sense for beauty, and touched
with emotion by being so put; not
thus put for us, and therefore, to the
majority of mankind, after a certain
while, unsatisfying, wearying.

Not to the born naturalist, I admit.
But what do we mean by a born naturalist? We mean a man in whom
the zeal for observing nature is so un-
commonly strong and eminent, that it
marks him off from the bulk of mankind. Such a man will pass his life

happily in collecting natural knowledge and reasoning upon it, and will
ask for nothing, or hardly anything,
more. I have heard it said that the
sagacious and admirable naturalist
whom we lost not very long ago, Mr.
Darwin, once owned to a friend that
for his part he did not experience the
necessity for two things which most
men find so necessary to them,—religion and poetry; science and the
domestic affections, he thought, were
enough. To a born naturalist, I can
well understand that this should seem
so. So absorbing is his occupation
with nature, so strong his love for his
occupation, that he goes on acquiring
natural knowledge and reasoning
upon it, and has little time or in-

clination for thinking about getting it related to the desire in man for conduct, the desire in man for beauty. He relates it to them for himself as he goes along, so far as he feels the need ; and he draws from the domestic affections all the additional solace necessary. But then Darwins are extremely rare. Another great and admirable master of natural knowledge, Faraday, was a Sandemanian. That is to say, he related his knowledge to his instinct for conduct and to his instinct for beauty, by the aid of that respectable Scottish sectary, Robert Sandeman. And so strong, in general, is the demand of religion and poetry to have their share in a man, to associate themselves with his knowing, and to relieve and rejoice it, that, probably, for one man amongst us with the disposition to do as Darwin did in this respect, there are at least fifty with the disposition to do as Faraday.

Education lays hold upon us, in fact, by satisfying this demand. Professor Huxley holds up to scorn mediæval education, with its neglect of the knowledge of nature, its poverty even of literary studies, its formal logic devoted to 'showing how and why that which the Church said was true must be true.' But the great mediæval Universities were not brought into being, we may be sure, by the zeal for giving a jejune and contemptible education. Kings have been their nursing fathers, and queens have been their nursing mothers, but not for this. The mediæval Universities came into being, because the supposed knowledge, delivered by Scripture and the Church, so deeply engaged men's hearts, by so simply, easily, and powerfully relating itself to their desire for conduct, their desire for beauty. All other knowledge was dominated by this supposed knowledge and was subordinated to it, because of the surpassing strength of the hold which it gained upon the affections of men, by allying itself profoundly with their sense for conduct, their sense for beauty.

But now, says Professor Huxley, conceptions of the universe fatal to

the notions held by our forefathers
have been forced upon us by physical
science. Grant to him that they are
thus fatal, that the new conceptions
must and will soon become current
everywhere, and that every one will
finally perceive them to be fatal to
the beliefs of our forefathers. The
need of humane letters, as they are
truly called, because they serve the
paramount desire in men that good
should be for ever present to them,
—the need of humane letters, to
establish a relation between the new
conceptions, and our instinct for
beauty, our instinct for conduct, is
only the more visible. The Middle
Age could do without humane letters,
as it could do without the study of

nature, because its supposed knowledge was made to engage its emotions so powerfully. Grant that the
supposed knowledge disappears, its
power of being made to engage the
emotions will of course disappear
along with it,—but the emotions themselves, and their claim to be engaged
and satisfied, will remain. Now if
we find by experience that humane
letters have an undeniable power of
engaging the emotions, the importance of humane letters in a man's
training becomes not less, but greater,
in proportion to the success of modern
science in extirpating what it calls
'mediæval thinking.'

Have humane letters, then, have
poetry and eloquence, the power here

attributed to them of engaging the
emotions, and do they exercise it?
And if they have it and exercise it,
how do they exercise it, so as to
exert an influence upon man's sense
for conduct, his sense for beauty?
Finally, even if they both can and do
exert an influence upon the senses
in question, how are they to relate
to them the results,—the modern
results,—of natural science? All
these questions may be asked.
First, have poetry and eloquence
the power of calling out the emotions? The appeal is to experience.
Experience shows that for the vast
majority of men, for mankind in
general, they have the power. Next,
do they exercise it? They do. But

then, *how* do they exercise it so as
to affect man's sense for conduct, his
sense for beauty? And this is perhaps a case for applying the Preacher's
words : 'Though a man labour to
seek it out, yet he shall not find it;
yea, farther, though a wise man think
to know it, yet shall he not be able
to find it.'[1] Why should it be one
thing, in its effect upon the emotions,
to say, 'Patience is a virtue,' and
quite another thing, in its effect upon
the emotions, to say with Homer,

τλητὸν γὰρ Μοῖραι θυμὸν θέσαν ἀνθρώποισιν—[2]

'for an enduring heart have the
destinies appointed to the children
of men'? Why should it be one

---

[1] *Ecclesiastes*, viii. 17.   [2] *Iliad*, xxiv. 49.

thing, in its effect upon the emotions,
to say with the philosopher Spinoza,
Felicitas in eo consistit quod homo
suum esse conservare potest—'Man's
happiness consists in his being able
to preserve his own essence,' and
quite another thing, in its effect upon
the emotions, to say with the Gospel,
'What is a man advantaged, if he
gain the whole world, and lose himself, forfeit himself?' How does this
difference of effect arise? I cannot
tell, and I am not much concerned to
know; the important thing is that it
does arise, and that we can profit by
it. But how, finally, are poetry and
eloquence to exercise the power of
relating the modern results of natural
science to man's instinct for conduct,

his instinct for beauty? And here
again I answer that I do not know
how they will exercise it, but that
they can and will exercise it I am
sure. I do not mean that modern
philosophical poets and modern philosophical moralists are to come and
relate for us, in express terms, the
results of modern scientific research
to our instinct for conduct, our instinct for beauty. But I mean that
we shall find, as a matter of experience, if we know the best that has
been thought and uttered in the
world, we shall find that the art and
poetry and eloquence of men who
lived, perhaps, long ago, who had
the most limited natural knowledge,
who had the most erroneous concep-

tions about many important matters,
we shall find that this art, and poetry,
and eloquence, have in fact not only
the power of refreshing and delighting us, they have also the power,—
such is the strength and worth, in
essentials, of their authors' criticism
of life,—they have a fortifying, and
elevating, and quickening, and sug-
gestive power, capable of wonderfully
helping us to relate the results of
modern science to our need for conduct, our need for beauty. Homer's
conceptions of the physical universe
were, I imagine, grotesque ; but
really, under the shock of hearing
from modern science that ' the world
is not subordinated to man's use, and
that man is not the cynosure of things

terrestrial,' I could, for my own part,
desire no better comfort than Homer's
line which I quoted just now,

τλητὸν γὰρ Μοῖραι θυμὸν θέσαν ἀνθρώποισιν—

'for an enduring heart have the destinies appointed to the children of
men'!

And the more that men's minds are
cleared, the more that the results of
science are frankly accepted, the more
that poetry and eloquence come to be
received and studied as what in truth
they really are,—the criticism of life
by gifted men, alive and active with
extraordinary power at an unusual
number of points;—so much the more
will the value of humane letters, and
of art also, which is an utterance having a like kind of power with theirs,

be felt and acknowledged, and their place in education be secured.

Let us therefore, all of us, avoid indeed as much as possible any invidious comparison between the merits of humane letters, as means of education, and the merits of the natural sciences. But when some President of a Section for Mechanical Science insists on making the comparison, and tells us that 'he who in his training has substituted literature and history for natural science has chosen the less useful alternative,' let us make answer to him that the student of humane letters only, will, at least, know also the great general conceptions brought in by modern physical science; for science, as Professor Huxley says,

forces them upon us all. But the
student of the natural sciences only,
will, by our very hypothesis, know
nothing of humane letters; not to
mention that in setting himself to
be perpetually accumulating natural
knowledge, he sets himself to do what
only specialists have in general the
gift for doing genially. And so he
will probably be unsatisfied, or at any
rate incomplete, and even more incomplete than the student of humane
letters only.

I once mentioned in a school-report,
how a young man in one of our English
training colleges having to paraphrase
the passage in *Macbeth* beginning,

'Can'st thou not minister to a mind diseased?'

turned this line into, ' Can you not wait

upon the lunatic?' And I remarked
what a curious state of things it would
be, if every pupil of our national schools
knew, let us say, that the moon is two
thousand one hundred and sixty miles
in diameter, and thought at the same
time that a good paraphrase for
'Can'st thou not minister to a mind diseased?'
was, 'Can you not wait upon the
lunatic?' If one is driven to choose,
I think I would rather have a young
person ignorant about the moon's
diameter, but aware that 'Can you not
wait upon the lunatic?' is bad, than
a young person whose education had
been such as to manage things the
other way.

Or to go higher than the pupils of
our national schools. I have in my

mind's eye a member of our British
Parliament who comes to travel here
in America, who afterwards relates
his travels, and who shows a really
masterly knowledge of the geology of
this great country and of its mining
capabilities, but who ends by gravely
suggesting that the United States
should borrow a prince from our
Royal Family, and should make him
their king, and should create a House
of Lords of great landed proprietors
after the pattern of ours; and then
America, he thinks, would have her
future happily and perfectly secured.
Surely, in this case, the President of
the Section for Mechanical Science
would himself hardly say that our
member of Parliament, by concentrat-

ing himself upon geology and miner-
alogy, and so on, and not attending
to literature and history, had 'chosen
the more useful alternative.'

If then there is to be separation
and option between humane letters
on the one hand, and the natural
sciences on the other, the great
majority of mankind, all who have
not exceptional and overpowering
aptitudes for the study of nature,
would do well, I cannot but think, to
choose to be educated in humane
letters rather than in the natural
sciences. Letters will call out their
being at more points, will make them
live more.

I said that before I ended I would
just touch on the question of classical

education, and I will keep my word.
Even if literature is to retain a large
place in our education, yet Latin and
Greek, say the friends of progress,
will certainly have to go. Greek is
the grand offender in the eyes of
these gentlemen. The attackers of
the established course of study think
that against Greek, at any rate, they
have irresistible arguments. Literature may perhaps be needed in education, they say; but why on earth
should it be Greek literature? Why
not French or German? Nay, 'has
not an Englishman models in his own
literature of every kind of excellence?
As before, it is not on any weak plead-
ings of my own that I rely for con-
vincing the gainsayers; it is on the

constitution of human nature itself, and on the instinct of self-preservation in humanity. The instinct for beauty is set in human nature, as surely as the instinct for knowledge is set there, or the instinct for conduct. If the instinct for beauty is served by Greek literature and art as it is served by no other literature and art, we may trust to the instinct of self-preservation in humanity for keeping Greek as part of our culture. We may trust to it for even making the study of Greek more prevalent than it is now. Greek will come, I hope, some day to be studied more rationally than at present; but it will be increasingly studied as men increasingly feel the need in them for beauty, and how

powerfully Greek art and Greek literature can serve this need.   Women
will again study Greek, as Lady Jane
Grey did ; I believe that in that chain
of forts, with which the fair host of
the Amazons are now engirdling our
English universities, I find that here
in America, in colleges like Smith
College in Massachusetts, and Vassar
College in the State of New York,
and in the happy families of the
mixed universities out West, they are
studying it already.

Defuit una mihi symmetria prisca,
—' The antique symmetry was the one
thing wanting to me,' said Leonardo da
Vinci ; and he was an Italian.   I will
not presume to speak for the Americans, but I am sure that, in the Eng-

lishman, the want of this admirable symmetry of the Greeks is a thousand times more great and crying than in any Italian. The results of the want show themselves most glaringly, perhaps, in our architecture, but they show themselves, also, in all our art. *Fit details strictly combined, in view of a large general result nobly conceived;* that is just the beautiful *symmetria prisca* of the Greeks, and it is just where we English fail, where all our art fails. Striking ideas we have, and well-executed details we have; but that high symmetry which, with satisfying and delightful effect, combines them, we seldom or never have. The glorious beauty of the Acropolis at Athens did not come from single fine things

stuck about on that hill, a statue here,
a gateway there;—no, it arose from
all things being perfectly combined
for a supreme total effect. What
must not an Englishman feel about
our deficiencies in this respect, as the
sense for beauty, whereof this symmetry is an essential element, awakens
and strengthens within him! what will
not one day be his respect and desire
for Greece and its *symmetria prisca*,
when the scales drop from his eyes as
he walks the London streets, and he
sees such a lesson in meanness as the
Strand, for instance, in its true de-
formity! But here we are coming to
our friend Mr. Ruskin's province, and
I will not intrude upon it, for he is its
very sufficient guardian.

And so we at last find, it seems, we find flowing in favour of the humanities the natural and necessary stream of things, which seemed against them when we started. The 'hairy quadruped furnished with a tail and pointed ears, probably arboreal in his habits,' this good fellow carried hidden in his nature, apparently, something destined to develop into a necessity for humane letters. Nay, more ; we seem finally to be even led to the further conclusion that our hairy ancestor carried in his nature, also, a necessity for Greek.

And therefore, to say the truth, I cannot really think that humane letters are in much actual danger of being thrust out from their leading place in education, in spite of

the array of authorities against them
at this moment. So long as human
nature is what it is, their attractions
will remain irresistible. As with
Greek, so with letters generally : they
will some day come, we may hope,
to be studied more rationally, but they
will not lose their place. What will
happen will rather be that there will
be crowded into education other matters besides, far too many ; there will
be, perhaps, a period of unsettlement
and confusion and false tendency ;
but letters will not in the end lose
their leading place. If they lose it
for a time, they will get it back again.
We shall be brought back to them by
our wants and aspirations. And a
poor humanist may possess his soul

in patience, neither strive nor cry,
admit the energy and brilliancy of
the partisans of physical science, and
their present favour with the public,
to be far greater than his own, and
still have a happy faith that the nature
of things works silently on behalf of
the studies which he loves, and that,
while we shall all have to acquaint ourselves with the great results reached
by modern science, and to give ourselves as much training in its disciplines as we can conveniently carry,
yet the majority of men will always
require humane letters; and so much
the more, as they have the more and
the greater results of science to relate
to the need in man for conduct, and
to the need in him for beauty.

EMERSON

FORTY years ago, when I was an
undergraduate at Oxford, voices were
in the air there which haunt my
memory still. Happy the man who
in that susceptible season of youth
hears such voices! they are a possession to him for ever. No such voices
as those which we heard in our youth
at Oxford are sounding there now.
Oxford has more criticism now, more
knowledge, more light; but such
voices as those of our youth it has

no longer. The name of Cardinal Newman is a great name to the imagination still; his genius and his style are still things of power. But he is over eighty years old; he is in the Oratory at Birmingham; he has adopted, for the doubts and difficulties which beset men's minds to-day, a solution which, to speak frankly, is impossible. Forty years ago he was in the very prime of life; he was close at hand to us at Oxford; he was preaching in St. Mary's pulpit every Sunday; he seemed about to transform and to renew what was for us the most national and natural institution in the world, the Church of England. Who could resist the charm of that spiritual apparition, gliding in

the dim afternoon light through the
aisles of St. Mary's, rising into the
pulpit, and then, in the most entranc-
ing of voices, breaking the silence
with words and thoughts which were
a religious music,—subtle, sweet,
mournful? I seem to hear him still,
saying : 'After the fever of life, after
wearinesses and sicknesses, fightings
and despondings, languor and fretful-
ness, struggling and succeeding ; after
all the changes and chances of this
troubled, unhealthy state,—at length
comes death, at length the white
throne of God, at length the beatific
vision.' Or, if we followed him back
to his seclusion at Littlemore, that
dreary village by the London road,
and to the house of retreat and the

church which he built there,—a mean
house such as Paul might have lived
in when he was tent-making at Ephesus, a church plain and thinly sown
with worshippers,—who could resist
him there either, welcoming back to
the severe joys of church-fellowship,
and of daily worship and prayer, the
firstlings of a generation which had
well-nigh forgotten them? Again I
seem to hear him: 'The season is chill
and dark, and the breath of the morn-
ing is damp, and worshippers are few;
but all this befits those who are by their
profession penitents and mourners,
watchers and pilgrims. More dear to
them that loneliness, more cheerful
that severity, and more bright that
gloom, than all those aids and ap-

pliances of luxury by which men
nowadays attempt to make prayer
less disagreeable to them. True
faith does not covet comforts; they
who realise that awful day, when
they shall see Him face to face
whose eyes are as a flame of fire,
will as little bargain to pray plea-
santly now as they will think of doing
so then.'

Somewhere or other I have spoken
of those 'last enchantments of the
Middle Age' which Oxford sheds
around us, and here they were! But
there were other voices sounding in
our ear besides Newman's. There
was the puissant voice of Carlyle; so
sorely strained, over-used, and mis-
used since, but then fresh, compara-

tively sound, and reaching our hearts
with true, pathetic eloquence. Who
can forget the emotion of receiving in
its first freshness such a sentence as
that sentence of Carlyle upon Edward
Irving, then just dead : 'Scotland sent
him forth a herculean man ; our mad
Babylon wore and wasted him with
all her engines,— and it took her
twelve years!' A greater voice still,
—the greatest voice of the century,—
came to us in those youthful years
through Carlyle : the voice of Goethe.
To this day,—such is the force of
youthful associations,—I read the
Wilhelm Meister with more pleasure
in Carlyle's translation than in the
original. The large, liberal view of
human life in *Wilhelm Meister*, how

novel it was to the Englishman in those days! and it was salutary, too, and educative for him, doubtless, as well as novel. But what moved us most in *Wilhelm Meister* was that which, after all, will always move the young most,—the poetry, the eloquence. Never, surely, was Carlyle's prose so beautiful and pure as in his rendering of the Youths' dirge over Mignon!—'Well is our treasure now laid up, the fair image of the past. Here sleeps it in the marble, undecaying; in your hearts, also, it lives, it works. Travel, travel, back into life! Take along with you this holy earnestness, for earnestness alone makes life eternity.' Here we had the voice of the great Goethe;—not the stiff, and hindered, and frigid, and factitious Goethe who speaks to us too often from those sixty volumes of his, but of the great Goethe, and the true one.

And besides those voices, there came to us in that old Oxford time a voice also from this side of the Atlantic,—a clear and pure voice, which for my ear, at any rate, brought a strain as new, and moving, and unforgettable, as the strain of Newman, or Carlyle, or Goethe. Mr. Lowell has well described the apparition of Emerson to your young generation here, in that distant time of which I am speaking, and of his workings upon them. He was your Newman, your man of soul and genius visible

to you in the flesh, speaking to your
bodily ears, a present object for your
heart and imagination. That is surely
the most potent of all influences!
nothing can come up to it. To us
at Oxford Emerson was but a voice
speaking from three thousand miles
away. But so well he spoke, that
from that time forth Boston Bay and
Concord were names invested to my
ear with a sentiment akin to that
which invests for me the names of
Oxford and of Weimar; and snatches
of Emerson's strain fixed themselves
in my mind as imperishably as any of
the eloquent words which I have been
just now quoting. 'Then dies the
man in you; then once more perish
the buds of art, poetry, and science,

as they have died already in a thousand thousand men.' 'What Plato
has thought, he may think ; what a
saint has felt, he may feel; what at
any time has befallen any man, he can
understand.'   'Trust thyself! every
heart vibrates to that iron string.
Accept the place the Divine Provi-
dence has found for you, the society
of your contemporaries, the connexion of events.   Great men have
always done so, and confided themselves childlike to the genius of their
age; betraying their perception that
the Eternal was stirring at their heart,
working through their hands, pre-
dominating in all their being.   And
we are now men, and must accept
in the highest spirit the same tran-

scendent destiny ; and not pinched in a corner, not cowards fleeing before a revolution, but redeemers and bene-factors, pious aspirants to be noble clay plastic under the Almighty effort, let us advance and advance on chaos and the dark ! '   These lofty sentences of Emerson, and a hundred others of like strain, I never have lost out of my memory ; I never *can* lose them.

At last I find myself in Emerson's own country, and looking upon Boston Bay.   Naturally I revert to the friend of my youth.   It is not always pleas-ant to ask oneself questions about the friends of one's youth ; they cannot always well support it.   Carlyle, for instance, in my judgment, cannot well support such a return upon him.   Yet

we should make the return ; we should
part with our illusions, we should
know the truth. When I come to
this country, where Emerson now
counts for so much, and where such
high claims are made for him, I pull
myself together, and ask myself what
the truth about this object of my
youthful admiration really is. Im-
proper elements often come into our
estimate of men. We have lately
seen a German critic make Goethe
the greatest of all poets, because
Germany is now the greatest of military powers, and wants a poet to
match. Then, too, America is a young
country ; and young countries, like
young persons, are apt sometimes to
evince in their literary judgments a

want of scale and measure. I set
myself, therefore, resolutely to come
at a real estimate of Emerson, and
with a leaning even to strictness
rather than to indulgence. That is
the safer course. Time has no indulgence ; any veils of illusion which
we may have left around an object
because we loved it, Time is sure to
strip away.

I was reading the other day a
notice of Emerson by a serious and
interesting American critic. Fifty or
sixty passages in Emerson's poems,
says this critic,—who had doubtless
himself been nourished on Emerson's
writings, and held them justly dear,—
fifty or sixty passages from Emer-

son's poems have already entered into
English speech as matter of familiar
and universally current quotation.
Here is a specimen of that personal
sort of estimate which, for my part,
even in speaking of authors dear to
me, I would try to avoid. What is
the kind of phrase of which we may
fairly say that it has entered into
English speech as matter of familiar
quotation? Such a phrase, surely,
as the 'Patience on a monument'
of Shakespeare; as the 'Darkness
visible' of Milton; as the 'Where
ignorance is bliss' of Gray. Of not
one single passage in Emerson's
poetry can it be truly said that it
has become a familiar quotation like
phrases of this kind. It is not

enough that it should be familiar to
his admirers, familiar in New England, familiar even throughout the
United States; it must be familiar
to all readers and lovers of English
poetry. Of not more than one or
two passages in Emerson's poetry
can it, I think, be truly said, that
they stand ever - present in the
memory of even many lovers of
English poetry. A great number of
passages from his poetry are no doubt
perfectly familiar to the mind and
lips of the critic whom I have mentioned, and perhaps a wide circle
of American readers. But this is a
very different thing from being matter
of universal quotation, like the phrases
of the legitimate poets.

And, in truth, one of the legitimate
poets, Emerson, in my opinion, is
not. His poetry is interesting, it
makes one think; but it is not the
poetry of one of the born poets. I
say it of him with reluctance, although I am sure that he would
have said it of himself; but I say it
with reluctance, because I dislike
giving pain to his admirers, and because all my own wish, too, is to say
of him what is favourable. But I
regard myself, not as speaking to
please Emerson's admirers, not as
speaking to please myself; but rather,
I repeat, as communing with Time
and Nature concerning the productions of this beautiful and rare spirit,
and as resigning what of him is by

their unalterable decree touched with
caducity, in order the better to mark
and secure that in him which is immortal.

Milton says that poetry ought to be
simple, sensuous, impassioned. Well,
Emerson's poetry is seldom either
simple, or sensuous, or impassioned.
In general it lacks directness ; it
lacks concreteness ; it lacks energy.
His grammar is often embarrassed ;
in particular, the want of clearly-
marked distinction between the subject and the object of his sentence
is a frequent cause of obscurity in
him. A poem which shall be a plain,
forcible, inevitable whole he hardly
ever produces. Such good work as
the noble lines graven on the Concord

Monument is the exception with him;
such ineffective work as the 'Fourth
of July Ode' or the 'Boston Hymn'
is the rule.   Even passages and single
lines of thorough plainness and com-
manding force are rare in his poetry.
They exist, of course; but when we
meet with them they give us a slight
shock of surprise, so little has Emerson accustomed us to them.   Let me
have the pleasure of quoting one or
two of these exceptional passages :—

> ' So nigh is grandeur to our dust,
>   So near is God to man,
> When Duty whispers low, *Thou must*,
>   The youth replies, *I can*.'

Or again this :—

> ' Though love repine and reason chafe,
>   There came a voice without reply :

"'Tis man's perdition to be safe,
When for the truth he ought to die."

Excellent! but how seldom do we
get from him a strain blown so clearly
and firmly! Take another passage
where his strain has not only clear-
ness, it has also grace and beauty :—

' And ever, when the happy child
  In May beholds the blooming wild,
  And hears in heaven the bluebird sing,
  "Onward," he cries, "your baskets bring !
  In the next field is air more mild,
  And in yon hazy west is Eden's balmier
      spring." '

In the style and cadence here there
is a reminiscence, I think, of Gray;
at any rate the pureness, grace, and
beauty of these lines are worthy even
of Gray. But Gray holds his high
rank as a poet, not merely by the

beauty and grace of passages in his
poems ; not merely by a diction
generally pure in an age of impure
diction : he holds it, above all, by
the power and skill with which the
evolution of his poems is conducted.
Here is his grand superiority to
Collins, whose diction in his best
poem, the 'Ode to Evening,' is purer
than Gray's ; but then the 'Ode to
Evening' is like a river which loses
itself in the sand, whereas Gray's best
poems have an evolution sure and
satisfying. Emerson's 'Mayday,' from
which I just now quoted, has no real
evolution at all ; it is a series of
observations. And, in general, his
poems have no evolution. Take, for
example, his 'Titmouse.' Here he has

an excellent subject ; and his observation of Nature, moreover, is always
marvellously close and fine.   But
compare what he makes of his meeting with his titmouse with what
Cowper or Burns makes of the like
kind of incident!   One never quite
arrives at learning what the titmouse
actually did for him at all, though
one feels a strong interest and desire
to learn it ; but one is reduced to
guessing, and cannot be quite sure
that after all one has guessed right.
He is not plain and concrete enough,
—in other words, not poet enough,—
to be able to tell us.   And a failure
of this kind goes through almost all
his verse, keeps him amid symbolism
and allusion and the fringes of things,

and, in spite of his spiritual power, deeply impairs his poetic value. Through the inestimable virtue of concreteness, a simple poem like 'The Bridge' of Longfellow, or the 'School Days' of Mr. Whittier, is of more poetic worth, perhaps, than all the verse of Emerson.

I do not, then, place Emerson among the great poets. But I go further, and say that I do not place him among the great writers, the great men of letters. Who are the great men of letters? They are men like Cicero, Plato, Bacon, Pascal, Swift, Voltaire,—writers with, in the first place, a genius and instinct for style; writers whose prose is by a kind of native necessity true and

sound.   Now the style of Emerson,
like the style of his transcendentalist
friends and of the ' Dial ' so continually,
—the style of Emerson is capable of
falling into a strain like this, which
I take from the beginning of his
' Essay on Love ' : ' Every soul is a
celestial being to every other soul.
The heart has its sabbaths and jubi-
lees, in which the world appears as
a hymeneal feast, and all natural
sounds and the circle of the seasons
are erotic odes and dances.'   Emerson altered this sentence in the later
editions.   Like Wordsworth, he was
in later life fond of altering ; and in
general his later alterations, like those
of Wordsworth, are not improve-
ments.   He softened the passage in

question, however, though without
really mending it. I quote it in its
original and strongly-marked form.
Arthur Stanley used to relate that
about the year 1840, being in conversation with some Americans in
quarantine at Malta, and thinking to
please them, he declared his warm admiration for Emerson's 'Essays,' then
recently published. However, the
Americans shook their heads, and told
him that for home taste Emerson was
decidedly too *greeny*. We will hope,
for their sakes, that the sort of thing
they had in their heads was such writing as I have just quoted. Unsound
it is, indeed, and in a style almost
impossible to a born man of letters.

It is a curious thing, that quality

of style which marks the great writer,
the born man of letters. It resides
in the whole tissue of his work, and
of his work regarded as a composition for literary purposes. Brilliant
and powerful passages in a man's
writings do not prove his possession
of it; it lies in their whole tissue.
Emerson has passages of noble and
pathetic eloquence, such as those
which I quoted at the beginning;
he has passages of shrewd and felicitous wit; he has crisp epigram; he
has passages of exquisitely touched
observation of nature. Yet he is not
a great writer; his style has not the
requisite wholeness of good tissue.
Even Carlyle is not, in my judgment,
a great writer. He has surpassingly

powerful qualities of expression, far more powerful than Emerson's, and reminding one of the gifts of expression of the great poets,—of even Shakespeare himself. What Emerson so admirably says of Carlyle's 'devouring eyes and portraying hand,' 'those thirsty eyes, those portrait-eating, portrait-painting eyes of thine, those fatal perceptions,' is thoroughly true. What a description is Carlyle's of the first publisher of *Sartor Resartus*, 'to whom the idea of a new edition of *Sartor* is frightful, or rather ludicrous, unimaginable'; of this poor Fraser, in whose 'wonderful world of Tory pamphleteers, conservative Younger-brothers, Regent Street loungers,

Crockford gamblers, Irish Jesuits,
drunken reporters, and miscellaneous
unclean persons (whom nitre and
much soap will not wash clean), not
a soul has expressed the smallest
wish that way!' What a portrait,
again, of the well-beloved John Ster-
ling! 'One, and the best, of a small
class extant here, who, nigh drowning
in a black wreck of Infidelity (lighted
up by some glare of Radicalism only,
now growing *dim* too), and about to
perish, saved themselves into a Cole-
ridgian Shovel-Hattedness.' What
touches in the invitation of Emerson
to London! 'You shall see block-
heads by the million; Pickwick himself shall be visible,—innocent young
Dickens, reserved for a questionable

fate. The great Wordsworth shall
talk till you yourself pronounce him
to be a bore. Southey's complexion
is still healthy mahogany brown, with
a fleece of white hair, and eyes that
seem running at full gallop. Leigh
Hunt, man of genius in the shape of
a cockney, is my near neighbour,
with good humour and no common-
sense; old Rogers with his pale
head, white, bare, and cold as snow,
with those large blue eyes, cruel,
sorrowful, and that sardonic shelf
chin.' How inimitable it all is! And
finally, for one must not go on for
ever, this version of a London Sunday, with the public-houses closed
during the hours of divine service!
'It is silent Sunday; the populace

not yet admitted to their beer-shops,
till the respectabilities conclude their
rubric mummeries,— a much more
audacious feat than beer.' Yet even
Carlyle is not, in my judgment, to
be called a great writer; one cannot
think of ranking him with men like
Cicero and Plato and Swift and Voltaire.   Emerson freely promises to
Carlyle immortality for his histories.
They will not have it.   Why?   Because the materials furnished to him
by that devouring eye of his, and that
portraying hand, were not wrought
in and subdued by him to what his
work, regarded as a composition for
literary purposes, required.   Occur-
ring in conversation, breaking out in
familiar correspondence, they are mag-

nificent, inimitable; nothing more is
required of them; thus thrown out
anyhow, they serve their turn and
fulfil their function. And, therefore,
I should not wonder if really Carlyle
lived, in the long run, by such an invaluable record as that correspondence
between him and Emerson, of which
we owe the publication to Mr. Charles
Norton,—by this and not by his
works, as Johnson lives in Boswell,
not by his works. For Carlyle's
sallies, as the staple of a literary
work, become wearisome; and as
time more and more applies to Carlyle's works its stringent test, this
will be felt more and more. Shakespeare, Molière, Swift,—they, too, had,
like Carlyle, the devouring eye and

the portraying hand.   But they are
great literary masters, they are
supreme writers, because they knew
how to work into a literary composition their materials, and to subdue
them to the purposes of literary effect.
Carlyle is too wilful for this, too turbid,
too vehement.

You will think I deal in nothing
but negatives.   I have been saying
that Emerson is not one of the great
poets, the great writers.   He has not
their quality of style.   He is, however, the propounder of a philosophy.
The Platonic dialogues afford us the
example of exquisite literary form
and treatment given to philosophical
ideas.   Plato is at once a great literary man and a great philosopher.

If we speak carefully, we cannot call Aristotle or Spinoza or Kant great literary men, or their productions great literary works. But their work is arranged with such constructive power that they build a philosophy, and are justly called great philosophical writers. Emerson cannot, I think, be called with justice a great philosophical writer. He cannot build; his arrangement of philosophical ideas has no progress in it, no evolution; he does not construct a philosophy. Emerson himself knew the defects of his method, or rather want of method, very well; indeed, he and Carlyle criticise themselves and one another in a way which leaves little for any one else to do in the way of formulating their defects. Carlyle formulates perfectly the defects of his friend's poetic and literary production when he says of the ' Dial ' : ' For me it is too ethereal, speculative, theoretic ; I will have all things condense themselves, take shape and body, if they are to have my sympathy.' And, speaking of Emerson's orations, he says : ' I long to see some concrete Thing, some Event, Man's Life, American Forest, or piece of Creation, which this Emerson loves and wonders at, well *Emersonised,*—depictured by Emerson, filled with the life of Emerson, and cast forth from him, then to live by itself. If these orations balk me of this, how profitable soever they

may be for others, I will not love
them.'   Emerson himself formulates
perfectly the defect of his own philosophical productions when he speaks
of his 'formidable tendency to the
lapidary style.   I build my house of
boulders.'   'Here I sit and read and
write,' he says again, 'with very little
system, and, as far as regards composition, with the most fragmentary
result; paragraphs incomprehensible,
each sentence an infinitely repellent
particle.'   Nothing can be truer; and
the work of a Spinoza or Kant, of the
men who stand as great philosophical
writers, does not proceed in this
wise.

Some people will tell you that
Emerson's poetry, indeed, is too ab-

stract, and his philosophy too vague, but that his best work is his *English Traits*. The *English Traits* are beyond question very pleasant reading. It is easy to praise them, easy to commend the author of them. But I insist on always trying Emerson's work by the highest standards. I esteem him too much to try his work by any other. Tried by the highest standards, and compared with the work of the excellent markers and recorders of the traits of human life,—of writers like Montaigne, La Bruyère, Addison,—the *English Traits* will not stand the comparison. Emerson's observation has not the disinterested quality of the observation of these masters. It is the observation of

a man systematically benevolent, as
Hawthorne's observation in *Our Old
Home* is the work of a man chagrined.
Hawthorne's literary talent is of the
first order.   His subjects are generally not to me subjects of the highest
interest ; but his literary talent is of
the first order, the finest, I think,
which America has yet produced, —
finer, by much, than Emerson's.   Yet
Our Old Home is not a masterpiece
any more than *English Traits*.   In
neither of them is the observer disinterested enough.   The author's attitude in each of these cases can easily
be understood and defended.   Hawthorne was a sensitive man, so situated
in England that he was perpetually
in contact with the British Philistine ;

and the British Philistine is a trying
personage.   Emerson's systematic benevolence comes from what he himself calls somewhere his 'persistent
optimism'; and his persistent optimism is the root of his greatness and
the source of his charm.   But still let
us keep our literary conscience true,
and judge every kind of literary work
by the laws really proper to it.   The
kind of work attempted in the *English
Traits* and in *Our Old Home* is work
which cannot be done perfectly with a
bias such as that given by Emerson's
optimism or by Hawthorne's chagrin.
Consequently, neither *English Traits*
nor *Our Old Home* is a work of perfection in its kind.

Not with the Miltons and Grays,

not with the Platos and Spinozas, not
with the Swifts and Voltaires, not
with the Montaignes and Addisons,
can we rank Emerson. His work of
various kinds, when one compares it
with the work done in a corresponding
kind by these masters, fails to stand
the comparison. No man could see
this clearer than Emerson himself. It
is hard not to feel despondency when
we contemplate our failures and shortcomings : and Emerson, the least self-
flattering and the most modest of
men, saw so plainly what was lacking
to him that he had his moments of
despondency. 'Alas, my friend,' he
writes in reply to Carlyle, who had
exhorted him to creative work,—'Alas,
my friend, I can do no such gay thing as

you say. I do not belong to the poets,
but only to a low department of literature,—the reporters; suburban men.'
He deprecated his friend's praise;
praise 'generous to a fault,' he calls
it; praise 'generous to the shaming
of me,—cold, fastidious, ebbing person
that I am. Already in a former letter
you had said too much good of my
poor little arid book, which is as sand
to my eyes. I can only say that I
heartily wish the book were better;
and I must try and deserve so much
favour from the kind gods by a bolder
and truer living in the months to
come,—such as may perchance one
day release and invigorate this cramp
hand of mine. When I see how
much work is to be done; what

room for a poet, for any spiritualist,
in this great, intelligent, sensual, and
avaricious America,—I lament my fumbling fingers and stammering tongue.'
Again, as late as 1870, he writes to
Carlyle: 'There is no example of
constancy like yours, and it always
stings my stupor into temporary re-
covery and wonderful resolution to
accept the noble challenge. But "the
strong hours conquer us;" and I am
the victim of miscellany,—miscellany
of designs, vast debility, and procras-
tination.' The forlorn note belonging
to the phrase, 'vast debility,' recalls
that saddest and most discouraged
of writers, the author of *Obermann*,
Senancour, with whom Emerson has
in truth a certain kinship. He has,

in common with Senancour, his pureness, his passion for nature, his single
eye; and here we find him confessing,
like Senancour, a sense in himself of
sterility and impotence.

And now I think I have cleared
the ground. I have given up to
envious Time as much of Emerson as
Time can fairly expect ever to obtain.
We have not in Emerson a great poet,
a great writer, a great philosophy-
maker. His relation to us is not that
of one of those personages; yet it is
a relation of, I think, even superior
importance. His relation to us is
more like that of the Roman Emperor
Marcus Aurelius. Marcus Aurelius
is not a great writer, a great philo-

sophy-maker; he is the friend and
aider of those who would live in the
spirit. Emerson is the same. He
is the friend and aider of those who
would live in the spirit. All the points
in thinking which are necessary for
this purpose he takes; but he does not
combine them into a system, or present them as a regular philosophy.
Combined in a system by a man with
the requisite talent for this kind of
thing, they would be less useful than as
Emerson gives them to us; and the
man with the talent so to systematise
them would be less impressive than
Emerson. They do very well as
they now stand;—like 'boulders,' as
he says;—in 'paragraphs incompress-
ible, each sentence an infinitely repel-

lent particle.' In such sentences his
main points recur again and again,
and become fixed in the memory.

We all know them. First and fore-
most, character. Character is everything. 'That which all things tend
to educe,—which freedom, cultivation,
intercourse, revolutions, go to form
and deliver,—is character.' Character
and self-reliance. 'Trust thyself!
every heart vibrates to that iron
string.' And yet we have our being
in a *not ourselves*. 'There is a power
above and behind us, and we are the
channels of its communications.' But
our lives must be pitched higher.
'Life must be lived on a higher plane;
we must go up to a higher platform, to
which we are always invited to ascend;

there the whole scene changes.' The
good we need is for ever close to us,
though we attain it not. 'On the
brink of the waters of life and truth,
we are miserably dying.' This good
is close to us, moreover, in our daily
life, and in the familiar, homely places.
'The unremitting retention of simple
and high sentiments in obscure duties,
—that is the maxim for us. Let us
be poised and wise, and our own to-
day. Let us treat the men and women
well,—treat them as if they were real;
perhaps they are. Men live in their
fancy, like drunkards whose hands
are too soft and tremulous for success-
ful labour. I settle myself ever firmer
in the creed, that we should not post-
pone and refer and wish, but do broad

justice where we are, by whomsoever we deal with; accepting our actual companions and circumstances, however humble or odious, as the mystic officials to whom the universe has delegated its whole pleasure for us. Massachusetts, Connecticut River, and Boston Bay, you think paltry places, and the ear loves names of foreign and classic topography. But here we are; and if we will tarry a little we may come to learn that here is best. See to it only that thyself is here.' Furthermore, the good is close to us *all*. 'I resist the scepticism of our education and of our educated men. I do not believe that the differences of opinion and character in men are organic. I do not recognise, besides

the class of the good and the wise, a
permanent class of sceptics, or a class
of conservatives, or of malignants, or
of materialists. I do not believe in
the classes. Every man has a call of
the power to do something unique.'
Exclusiveness is deadly. 'The ex-
clusive in social life does not see that
he excludes himself from enjoyment
in the attempt to appropriate it. The
exclusionist in religion does not see
that he shuts the door of heaven on
himself in striving to shut out others.
Treat men as pawns and ninepins, and
you shall suffer as well as they. If
you leave out their heart you shall
lose your own. The selfish man suffers
more from his selfishness than he
from whom that selfishness withholds

some important benefit.'   A sound
nature will be inclined to refuse ease
and self-indulgence.   'To live with
some rigour of temperance, or some
extreme of generosity, seems to be an
asceticism which common good-nature
would appoint to those who are at
ease and in plenty, in sign that they
feel a brotherhood with the great
multitude of suffering men.'   Com-
pensation, finally, is the great law of
life ; it is everywhere, it is sure, and
there is no escape from it.   This is
that 'law alive and beautiful, which
works over our heads and under our
feet.   Pitiless, it avails itself of our
success when we obey it, and of our
ruin when we contravene it.   We are
all secret believers in it.   It rewards

actions after their nature. The re-
ward of a thing well done is to have
done it. The thief steals from himself, the swindler swindles himself.
You must pay at last your own debt.'

This is tonic indeed! And let no
one object that it is too general; that
more practical, positive direction is
what we want; that Emerson's optimism, self-reliance, and indifference
to favourable conditions for our life
and growth have in them something
of danger. 'Trust thyself;' 'what
attracts my attention shall have it;'
'though thou shouldst walk the world
over thou shalt not be able to find a
condition inopportune or ignoble;'
'what we call vulgar society is that
society whose poetry is not yet written,

but which you shall presently make
as enviable and renowned as any.'
With maxims like these, we surely,
it may be said, run some risk of being
made too well satisfied with our own
actual self and state, however crude
and imperfect they may be. 'Trust
thyself?' It may be said that the
common American or Englishman is
more than enough disposed already to
trust himself. I often reply, when our
sectarians are praised for following
conscience : Our people are very
good in following their conscience ;
where they are not so good is in ascer-
taining whether their conscience tells
them right. 'What attracts my attention shall have it ?' Well, that is our
people's plea when they run after the

Salvation Army, and desire Messrs.
Moody and Sankey. ' Thou shalt not
be able to find a condition inopportune or ignoble ?' But think of the
turn of the good people of our race
for producing a life of hideousness and
immense ennui ; think of that specimen of your own New England life
which Mr. Howells gives us in one
of his charming stories which I was
reading lately ; think of the life of
that ragged New England farm in
the *Lady of the Aroostook ;* think of
Deacon Blood, and Aunt Maria, and
the straight-backed chairs with black
horse-hair seats, and Ezra Perkins
with perfect self-reliance depositing
his travellers in the snow ! I can
truly say that in the little which I

have seen of the life of New England,
I am more struck with what has been
achieved than with the crudeness and
failure. But no doubt there is still
a great deal of crudeness also. Your
own novelists say there is, and I suppose they say true. In the New
England, as in the Old, our people
have to learn, I suppose, not that
their modes of life are beautiful and
excellent already ; they have rather to
learn that they must transform them.

To adopt this line of objection to
Emerson's deliverances would, however, be unjust. In the first place,
Emerson's points are in themselves
true, if understood in a certain high
sense ; they are true and fruitful.
And the right work to be done, at

the hour when he appeared, was to affirm them generally and absolutely. Only thus could he break through the hard and fast barrier of narrow, fixed ideas, which he found confronting him, and win an entrance for new ideas. Had he attempted developments which may now strike us as expedient, he would have excited fierce antagonism, and probably effected little or nothing. The time might come for doing other work later, but the work which Emerson did was the right work to be done then.

In the second place, strong as was Emerson's optimism, and unconquerable as was his belief in a good result to emerge from all which he saw going on around him, no misanthro-

pical satirist ever saw shortcomings
and absurdities more clearly than he
did, or exposed them more courage-
ously.   When he sees 'the meanness,'
as he calls it, 'of American politics,'
he congratulates Washington on being
'long already happily dead,' on being
'wrapt in his shroud and for ever
safe.'   With how firm a touch he
delineates the faults of your two great
political parties of forty years ago!
The Democrats, he says, 'have not
at heart the ends which give to the
name of democracy what hope and
virtue are in it. The spirit of our
American radicalism is destructive and
aimless; it is not loving; it has no
ulterior and divine ends, but is destructive only out of hatred and self-

ishness. On the other side, the conservative party, composed of the most
moderate, able, and cultivated part of
the population, is timid, and merely
defensive of property. It vindicates
no right, it aspires to no real good, it
brands no crime, it proposes no generous policy. From neither party, when
in power, has the world any benefit to
expect in science, art, or humanity, at
all commensurate with the resources
of the nation.' Then with what subtle
though kindly irony he follows the
gradual withdrawal in New England,
in the last half century, of tender
consciences from the social organisa-
tions,—the bent for experiments such
as that of Brook Farm and the like,—
follows it in all its 'dissidence of dis-

sent and Protestantism of the Pro-
testant religion!' He even loves to
rally the New Englander on his phil-
anthropical activity, and to find his
beneficence and its institutions a bore!
'Your miscellaneous popular charities,
the education at college of fools, the
building of meeting-houses to the vain
end to which many of these now stand,
alms to sots, and the thousand-fold
relief societies,—though I confess with
shame that I sometimes succumb and
give the dollar, yet it is a wicked
dollar, which by and by I shall have
the manhood to withhold.' 'Our
Sunday schools and churches and
pauper societies are yokes to the
neck. We pain ourselves to please
nobody. There are natural ways of

arriving at the same ends at which
these aim, but do not arrive.' ' Nature
does not like our benevolence or our
learning much better than she likes
our frauds and wars. When we come
out of the caucus, or the bank, or the
Abolition convention, or the Temperance meeting, or the Transcendental
club, into the fields and woods,
she says to us: "So hot, my little
sir ? " '

Yes, truly, his insight is admirable ;
his truth is precious. Yet the secret
of his effect is not even in these ; it is
in his temper. It is in the hopeful,
serene, beautiful temper wherewith
these, in Emerson, are indissolubly
joined ; in which they work, and have
their being. He says himself: ' We

judge of a man's wisdom by his hope, knowing that the perception of the inexhaustibleness of nature is an immortal youth.' If this be so, how wise is Emerson! for never had man such a sense of the inexhaustibleness of nature, and such hope. It was the ground of his being; it never failed him. Even when he is sadly avowing the imperfection of his literary power and resources, lamenting his fumbling fingers and stammering tongue, he adds: 'Yet, as I tell you, I am very easy in my mind and never dream of suicide. My whole philosophy, which is very real, teaches acquiescence and optimism. Sure I am that the right word will be spoken, though I cut out my tongue.' In his old age, with

friends dying and life failing, his tone
of cheerful, forward-looking hope is
still the same. ' A multitude of young
men are growing up here of high
promise, and I compare gladly the
social poverty of my youth with the
power on which these draw.' His
abiding word for us, the word by
which being dead he yet speaks to us,
is this: 'That which befits us, em-
bosomed in beauty and wonder as we
are, is cheerfulness and courage, and
the endeavour to realise our aspirations. Shall not the heart, which has
received so much, trust the Power by
which it lives?'

One can scarcely overrate the importance of thus holding fast to happiness and hope. It gives to Emer-

son's work an invaluable virtue. As
Wordsworth's poetry is, in my judgment, the most important work done
in verse, in our language, during the
present century, so Emerson's *Essays*
are, I think, the most important work
done in prose. His work is more
important than Carlyle's. Let us be
just to Carlyle, provoking though he
often is. Not only has he that genius
of his which makes Emerson say
truly of his letters, that 'they savour
always of eternity.' More than this
may be said of him. The scope and
upshot of his teaching are true; 'his
guiding genius,' to quote Emerson
again, is really 'his moral sense,
his perception of the sole importance
of truth and justice.' But consider

Carlyle's temper, as we have been considering Emerson's! take his own account of it! 'Perhaps London is the proper place for me after all, seeing all places are *im*proper: who knows? Meanwhile, I lead a most dyspeptic, solitary, self-shrouded life; consuming, if possible in silence, my considerable daily allotment of pain; glad when any strength is left in me for writing, which is the only use I can see in myself,—too rare a case of late. The ground of my existence is black as death; too black, when all *void* too; but at times there paint themselves on it pictures of gold, and rainbow, and lightning; all the brighter for the black ground, I sup-pose. Withal, I am very much of a fool.'—No, not a fool, but turbid and morbid, wilful and perverse. 'We judge of a man's wisdom by his hope.'

Carlyle's perverse attitude towards happiness cuts him off from hope. He fiercely attacks the desire for happiness; his grand point in *Sartor*, his secret in which the soul may find rest, is that one shall cease to desire happiness, that one should learn to say to oneself: 'What if thou wert born and predestined not to be happy, but to be unhappy!' He is wrong; Saint Augustine is the better philosopher, who says: 'Act we *must* in pursuance of what gives us most delight.' Epictetus and Augustine can be severe moralists enough; but both of them know and frankly say that the desire for happiness is the root and ground of man's being. Tell him and show him that he places his happiness wrong, that he seeks for delight where delight will never be really found; then you illumine and further him. But you only confuse him by telling him to cease to desire happiness : and you will not tell him this unless you are already confused yourself.

Carlyle preached the dignity of labour, the necessity of righteousness, the love of veracity, the hatred of shams. He is said by many people to be a great teacher, a great helper for us, because he does so. But what is the due and eternal result of labour, righteousness, veracity ?—

Happiness. And how are we drawn
to them by one who, instead of making us feel that with them is happiness, tells us that perhaps we were
predestined not to be happy but to
be unhappy ?

You will find, in especial, many
earnest preachers of our popular religion to be fervent in their praise and
admiration of Carlyle. His insistence
on labour, righteousness, and veracity, pleases them; his contempt for
happiness pleases them too. I read
the other day a tract against smoking,
although I do not happen to be a
smoker myself. 'Smoking,' said the
tract, ' is liked because it gives agreeable sensations. Now it is a positive
objection to a thing that it gives

agreeable sensations. An earnest man
will expressly avoid what gives agreeable sensations.' Shortly afterwards
I was inspecting a school, and I found
the children reading a piece of poetry
on the common theme that we are
here to-day and gone to-morrow. I
shall soon be gone, the speaker in this
poem was made to say,—

> ' And I shall be glad to go,
>> For the world at best is a dreary place,
>> And my life is getting low.'

How usual a language of popular
religion that is, on our side of the
Atlantic at any rate! But then our
popular religion, in disparaging happiness here below, knows very well
what it is after. It has its eye on a
happiness in a future life above the

clouds, in the New Jerusalem, to be
won by disliking and rejecting happiness here on earth. And so long as
this ideal stands fast, it is very well.
But for very many it now stands fast
no longer; for Carlyle, at any rate, it
had failed and vanished. Happiness
in labour, righteousness, and veracity,
—in the life of the spirit,—here was
a gospel still for Carlyle to preach,
and to help others by preaching.
But he baffled them and himself by
preferring the paradox that we are not
born for happiness at all.

Happiness in labour, righteousness,
and veracity; in all the life of the
spirit; happiness and eternal hope;—
that was Emerson's gospel. I hear it
said that Emerson was too sanguine;

that the actual generation in America
is not turning out so well as he
expected. Very likely he was too
sanguine as to the near future; in
this country it is difficult not to be
too sanguine. Very possibly the present generation may prove unworthy
of his high hopes; even several gene-
rations succeeding this may prove
unworthy of them. But by his conviction that in the life of the spirit is
happiness, and by his hope that this
life of the spirit will come more and
more to be sanely understood, and to
prevail, and to work for happiness,—
by this conviction and hope Emerson
was great, and he will surely prove in
the end to have been right in them.
In this country it is difficult, as I

said, not to be sanguine. Very many
of your writers are over-sanguine,
and on the wrong grounds. But you
have two men who in what they have
written show their sanguineness in a
line where courage and hope are just,
where they are also infinitely important, but where they are not easy.
The two men are Franklin and
Emerson.[1] These two are, I think,

[1] I found with pleasure that this conjunction
of Emerson's name with Franklin's had already
occurred to an accomplished writer and delightful
man, a friend of Emerson, left almost the sole
survivor, alas! of the famous literary generation
of Boston,—Dr. Oliver Wendell Holmes. Dr.
Holmes has kindly allowed me to print here the ingenious and interesting lines, hitherto unpublished,
in which he speaks of Emerson thus :—

> ' Where in the realm of thought, whose air is song,
> Does he, the Buddha of the West, belong?
> He seems a wingéd Franklin, sweetly wise,
> Born to unlock the secret of the skies ;

the most distinctively and honourably
American of your writers; they are
the most original and the most valuable. Wise men everywhere know
that we must keep up our courage
and hope; they know that hope is,
as Wordsworth well says,—

' The paramount *duty* which Heaven lays,
  For its own honour, on man's suffering heart.'

But the very word *duty* points to an
effort and a struggle to maintain our
hope unbroken. Franklin and Emerson maintained theirs with a convin-
cing ease, an inspiring joy. Franklin's
confidence in the happiness with

      And which the nobler calling—if 'tis fair
      Terrestrial with celestial to compare—
      To guide the storm-cloud's elemental flame,
      Or walk the chambers whence the lightning came
      Amidst the sources of its subtile fire,
      And steal their effluence for his lips and lyre?'

which industry, honesty, and economy
will crown the life of this work-day
world, is such that he runs over with
felicity. With a like felicity does
Emerson run over, when he con-
templates the happiness eternally attached to the true life in the spirit.
You cannot prize him too much, nor
heed him too diligently. He has
lessons for both the branches of our
race. I figure him to my mind as
visible upon earth still, as still standing here by Boston Bay, or at his
own Concord, in his habit as he
lived, but of heightened stature and
shining feature, with one hand
stretched out towards the East, to
our laden and labouring England;
the other towards the ever-growing

West, to his own dearly - loved
America,—'great, intelligent, sensual,
avaricious America.' To us he shows
for guidance his lucid freedom, his
cheerfulness and hope ; to you his
dignity, delicacy, serenity, elevation.

THE END

Printed by R. & R. CLARK, LIMITED, *Edinburgh.*